RISE

```
get unstuck.
make a change.
```

karen gunton

karen gunton

karengunton.com

copyright © karen gunton 2020

ISBN 978-0-9945646-6-5

the moral rights of the author have been asserted. the stories, suggestions and opinions of the author are personal views only. the strategies and steps outlined are a guide only. the author in all cases recommends personal due diligence and thorough research. all rights reserved. this book may not be reproduced in whole, part, stored, posted on in the internet or transmitted in any form by any means, electronic, mechanical, photocopying, recording, or other without the written permission from the author.

cover design: karen gunton

cover image: CC0 public domain pixabay.com author: giselafotografie

author photo: karen gunton

printed by: ingramspark.com

dedication.

for my mom

leanne dutka haltiner

you were stuck for so long. you had so many things you still longed to do. you ran out of time. in your name, i make a promise to help as many people as i can to get themselves unstuck so they can have the life they long for, do the things they dream of, and be exactly who they wish to be. life is too short for anything else.

with thanks to my dad

ken haltiner

you lived your life exactly how you wanted to... no excuses, no apologies. you had the biggest, most generous heart of anyone. and you reminded me in your final weeks and days that life is here for living. you were truly stuck... i just *felt* stuck. but i actually have everything i need to get unstuck and move forward and live a life that you and mom will be proud of.

rise.

our stuckness is like a box...

it keeps us small, safe, same, still, and silent.

when we shift the box...

we can RISE.

forward.

The broken in cushions of your couch. The heavy comfort of down feathers on a king size bed. For me it was a worn out rug. on my office floor and a popcorn ceiling that stared back at me for hours. We all have a place where we go. To sink. Our place to turn it all off. Or convince ourselves we're trying to. We like to think it's comfortable there. That it's safe. Only it's not.

It's stagnant.

It's a trap.

And we built it ourselves.

Getting up just to lay back down again can become an easy habit to justify. Especially when doing anything else seems so triumphantly hard. Outside there are voices barking, too many, too loud. Or just the opposite; a silence that's heavy and lonely. Expectations. People don't understand. People understand so much you can't relate. Or don't want to. You are always alone. Inside your head is the real battle. Your own voice telling you *no, there's no point*, aching for you to stay where you are. That's the one you listen to most.

Getting up when you're down is the biggest of internal battles. We make it worse without realizing. We make excuses. We lie to ourselves. We're not good enough. We're not ready. We want someone to tell us what to do because the thought of us knowing on our own is so incredibly daunting. What if we're wrong? What if we fail?

The thing is, and it's a big one, there is no yes or no or right or wrong. There is only you. Actually making a choice to get up again. Rising is not about coming out of the ashes an all mighty powerful Phoenix, suddenly triumphant and unstoppable. It's about taking steps. Little steps that say: *Yes. I'm going to. I can.* No is such an easy word to tell ourselves, but all it does is stop us. And it's pointless. Because it only pretends to keep us safe.

No matter what it is that got you where you are, make no mistake, you're allowed to lie down. You're allowed to feel lost and unsure, wounded and weak. You're allowed to sink. You're just not allowed to stay there.

Getting up again can feel like the tallest mountain to climb. But it's just about taking a little step. And then another.

Say yes.

Make a choice.

You're already reading this book. That's a little step.

Bruce James

about this book.

as you will notice right away, this book does not contain capital letters. you may be wondering what the hell is up with that?

when i started writing and blogging in 2010 i really struggled at first to get my words on the page and nothing i wrote felt like me because i was trying to conform to all of these rules i had in my head about writing. i decided then and there to *just be me*. to write like i talk, to swear if i want to, and to not use capital letters. once i gave myself permission to be me, and to break the rules, the words started to flow.

since that day you will not find capital letters in anything i write, teach, create, or share. ever. anywhere. including this book. (well, unless i am doing SHOUTY caps. i like those caps.)

so, if i started using capital letters now – just because this is a real book book, one printed on actual paper with a glossy cover and everything – that would be a complete cop out, wouldn't it?

my message has always been that *you need to be YOU*. just as i need to be me. the whole premise of the lighthouse revolution – rising up and standing tall and shining bright and BEing a lighthouse – is that you deserve to own your light in the world and live a life that lights you up.

we RISE when we BE who we are and light up in whatever way we choose.

and so i will carry on shining my light in the way that feels like me, and i hope to inspire you to do the same.

now let's get unstuck.... let's RISE.

table of contents.

introduction: get unstuck	19
choose your own adventure.	27
practice self-leadership.	29
part one: awareness strategies	33
tools of awareness.	35
meet the lighthouse keepers.	47
meet your shadow hunter.	56
meet your inner child.	64
meet your future self.	68
the one BIG challenge.	74
the swinging pendulum.	80
the wreck.	86
the road so far.	90
the destination dream.	94
where else might this be true?	98
sticky steps.	101
play bingo.	106
look in the mirror.	111
body wisdom.	115
muscle test.	121
cycles & rhythms.	125

part two: shifting strategies	133
be intentional.	139
choose an anchor.	143
forgiveness.	148
cord cutting.	154
surrender.	161
tapping.	166
emotional release.	171
check your bucket.	176
word work.	180
sign a new contract.	184
pick a new job.	188
make good choices.	192
rewrite the story.	198
get physical.	205

part three: unstucking strategies 213
  jealousy.the light you see in others is a sign. 217
  hiding. know your zones. 220
  doubt. train your inner dragon. 224
  unworthy. celebrate good times. 230
  uncertain. what you know for sure. 235
  crickets. focus on ONE boat. 241
  meh. show up and help someone. 245
  failure. a new purpose. 248
  annoyed & irritated. hire an assistant. 253
  self-sabotage. build a safety net. 258
  worry. be where your feet are. 263
  overwhelm. choose ONE thing. 268
  disconnected. treasure hunt. 272
  insignificant. we've got work to do. 280
  shame. love yourself up. 284
  fear. stand inside the fire. 290
  lack. savvy spender 297
  no mojo. rebel yell. 303
  lost. choose your mission. 309
  yah, but... the ONE possibility. 314
  grief. feeling is healing. 317
  inertia. JFDI. just fucking do it. 324

conclusion: stepping forward	329
make it a thing.	333
track it.	337
a story: #selfielove challenge.	340
darkness is a black hole. take baby steps.	347
a story: water & savasana.	352
look to the sun.	358

preface.

i wrote this book during NaNoWriMo, november 2017. just a few months later, my life began to change... irrevocably.

on february 20 2018 i was at my desk, working on plans for the new year ahead, feeling energised and creative. (for me february is the new january!) the phone rang, my mom calling from canada to deliver heartbreaking news: my cousin had died, tragically, and could i please come home.

through the rest of 2018 i found myself falling into a deep depression. we decided to NOT move back to canada (which is what i had been envisioning and dreaming about), and this decision, after losing a family member and longing to go home again, created more grief than i expected. i deeply missed my family. my husband spent the year working and living in another city. we bought our first house. it was a lot.

on february 21 2019 i got another awful call from canada, my dad with the news that mom had terminal lung cancer.

ironically, i was sitting in the same spot when my dad called as i was the day, one year plus one day previous, when my mom had called with heartbreaking news. it was once again the start of a new year, i was finally feeling ignited again after the loss and the grief and the challenges of the previous year. and then my dad called, and everything changed... again.

i went home twice over the coming months to be with my mom for extended periods of time. i was there with her in hospice when she died on july 4th 2019.

six months later, on new year's day of 2020, just as i was beginning to feel like i was healing, i received yet another devastating phone call. my dad had a massive stroke.

i went home to be with him. and i am so fucking grateful for the time i had with each of my parents before they died. (note: if you ever get the call and wonder 'should i go or not?' the answer is yes, go. you won't ever regret going even if it is difficult and costly.)

when my mom died i felt like i had lost myself as well as losing her. when i sat with my dad after his stroke - he was alive and breathing and nodding his head yes and no, but he couldn't move and he couldn't talk and we didn't know if he could understand us - he reminded me that life is for living. i could no longer stay stuck in my head or my bed... dad was the one truly stuck, my stuckness could be shifted.

on february 15 2020, my dad had another stroke and died. the pain of losing him was excruciating, especially so soon after losing mom. but i do believe he is in a better place, and that comforts me.

sadly, on may 29 2020, my beloved grandad passed at 95 years of age. he was my actual hero. from him i learned about living life to its absolute fullest... experiencing every bit of adventure, love, and joy we can create. the gift of the previous trips to canada for each loss in our family provided me with more time with him... losing him felt like a closure in a way. after that, i pledged to once again begin the work of moving forward.

i still feel lost, i have no idea what to do or where i go now... but i can also move forward into whatever that is, knowing my parents gave me everything i need: strength, love, and unwavering support.

it has been a tough two years. my business basically shut down, i am suddenly an orphan feeling untethered in the world, and i lost my sense of purpose along the way. but i know i can find those things - business, purpose, and belonging - again.

at the start of a new year i used to think: 'yes! i am leaving that crap year behind! THIS is my year!' but now i think maybe the crap is just going to keep on happening, and i just need to get better at dealing and healing and moving forward.

and so this is how i came to revisit this book – about getting unstuck and rising – once again, nearly three years after i first wrote it.

you will learn about something i call 'the wreck' in an upcoming chapter; i believe i have experienced the wreck in a big way these past months. i have never felt more stuck than when i was trying to emerge from the depths of depression and grief, truly lost in the darkness. i have been using these strategies myself and discovered some new ones too.

as i do the work to finish this book and share it with the world, we are in the midst of a worldwide pandemic, isolated at home, with many people experiencing new levels of anxiety, stress, worry, overwhelm, grief, depression, dejection, frustration, fear, and sadness. this is a period of time that will change each of us – something different will be on the other side. and i know from experience that climbing out of that space can be tricky, so i hope that when people are ready, the strategies shared here will be simple, practical steps to help you move forward into whatever is next for you.

there is absolutely a time for grief, a time for quiet and stillness, a time for processing and just being. but then i think there comes a time where you feel ready... ready to emerge, ready to move forward, ready for change, or ready for the next steps.

after the darkness comes the RISING.

this book is for those of us feeling ready to RISE again.

rise. 18

introduction

rise. 20

get unstuck.

i believe that we are here to shine our light in the world. this is our purpose, it is what we were born to do... we are here to shine in whatever way we choose, in whatever way calls to us.

but i do find that the word *shine* is a bit overused in our world today... sometimes it feels like everyone is throwing it around.

"it's your time to shine!"

my brain asks: ok. but HOW?

my first book *lighthouse revolution* was a HOW.

i figured that if i wanted to shine, then i needed to build myself a lighthouse... i needed to BE a lighthouse.

lighthouse revolution is all about how to build up each component of our lighthouse so that we can indeed shine.

this book is a little different. it's about being our own lighthouse keeper and doing the ongoing maintenance that is required to keep shining.

many of us spend a lot of our lifetime exploring what ignites that light inside of us... we search for that sense of purpose, we chase after our dreams...

but there is more to 'shining' than being ignited. there is more work to do in our life time.

because even when we do indeed feel lit up inside there can be a layer of FOG that clouds over the windows of our lighthouse and prevents our light from shining through.

that 'fog' comes from all of the **fear, worry, doubt, lack, frustration, and overwhelm** we experience and all of the various ways that stuff shows up in our lives. clearing it away is part of our job here... in fact it is an ongoing job, one that never really ends.

and the truth is, this isn't easy work.

as we take this journey towards shining our light we can experience all kinds of stuckness. it can feel like a barrier is in the way — a block in our path, an obstacle we must overcome, some sort of resistance preventing us from moving forward — like a box that keeps us small, safe, same, silent, stuck.

we can feel ignited, we can have an idea of what we need to do in order to shine, we can even have an idea of what is getting in the way — what is fogging up the windows — but still feel *so very stuck* because we don't know HOW to change things or clear the stuff that is in our way. we aren't empowered with tools that work... it all feels too hard... and we stay stuck.

this book is the HOW. it offers the tools and strategies and ideas for cleaning those foggy windows, for getting unstuck, for creating a shift or making a change... for being your own leader and RISING out of the place you are in and into the place you want to be.

i have been searching for concrete HOWs — real strategies that we can actually use to work on our 'stuff' — for a long time. i have been learning and exploring and testing these strategies myself, and i want to share them with you.

this book is a little different to other 'self-help' type books that you will come across. i have written this as a *choose your own adventure* style of book because the truth is that we each have different kinds of 'stuff' fogging up our windows or blocking our path.

you care most about *your* stuff... the stuff that is causing you the most stuckness right now!

plus you will have *your* own way for working on your stuff... the way that suits you best! we are each different. you do you!

my background is teaching. i started my career path teaching science to kids and have been teaching in one form or another for over 20 years. i know that we all learn in different ways, that some strategies or tools will suit some and not others... i honour and, indeed, value our differences.

so my aim is to offer you a variety of strategies and tools that you can choose and try and apply to your stuff... i want you to feel empowered to take action in your own life to get unstuck and RISE up.

please note: this book and the strategies i am sharing here do not replace therapy, counselling, or medical intervention. if your particular brand of stuckness includes depression, anxiety, post-traumatic stress, suicidal thoughts, OCD, or any other mental health challenge, please seek professional help. i am not a trained mental health professional and i absolutely do not want to discount the enormity of anything you might be experiencing right now.

quite simply, i am a teacher. i am here to teach self-leadership strategies that i hope will help *you* to help yourself. i wish to offer strategies that you can do yourself, try yourself, practice yourself, and adapt yourself. each strategy shared here is something you can try out on your own, right away. if you find a strategy that resonates i do encourage you to learn more or practice further, and where possible i have included resources that can help you with that.

i want to make things click. i want this to be doable. i want you to have the tools you need to get unstuck and RISE up in one handy spot... so that you can actually do something about your stuckness and experience a real difference, instead of just talking about it or living with it or struggling with it on your own.

having said that, i acknowledge that i am writing this book very much aware of my own privilege — i have the space, support, time, money, ability, and safety to do this work on and for myself. i fully recognise that some challenges won't be overcome by simple self-help strategies with cutesy names. some of us are facing issues that go beyond being 'stuck' — systemic oppression, inequality, discrimination, and abuse; barriers trenched in race, gender, sexuality, religion, culture, ability, and more.

i honour the reality that many of us are facing some big challenges, ones that i do not wish to negate with the simple ideas shared in this book.

my hope is that no matter what we each are facing, this will be a book that will be a starting point, something you can build on, a way to help yourself in whatever stuck place you find yourself in - lost, inertia, doubt, lack, fear, frustration, etc — by working on your own personal thoughts, actions, beliefs, mindset, or energy.

if you can RISE from the stuckness you experience inside of you... you can better work on the stuckness you find around you.

if you can move forward with your own dreams, plans, and goals... you can shine your light in the way you choose.

the more of us that do that we have the greater capacity to change the world in bigger ways.

choose your own adventure.

here's how this book works...

part one includes strategies for awareness to explore and shine a light on whatever is fogging up your windows or leaving you feeling stuck in your path. you can't do the work to shift your stuff if you don't know exactly what is getting in your way!

part two includes general strategies for clearing that stuff. these general strategies are tools in your toolbelt that you can call upon and use for all kinds of stuckness, in all kinds of situations!

part three includes specific strategies to shift the exact things that you are experiencing right now: maybe it's a lack of confidence, maybe it's a lack of mojo, maybe it's something else!

what you can do with this book is choose an awareness strategy from part one, a clearing strategy from part two, and some specific help for your 'stuff' in part three... put them together, adapt them, or make them your own to create a doable, practical, and powerful strategy for yourself that will actually help you RISE out of your stuckness.

you might just want to skip ahead right now to whatever your personal brand of stuckness is... and you can definitely use this book in that way! but i do recommend reading through the whole book first to get an idea of the different strategies you can use. i hope to plant the seeds in your mind so that you know they are here for you to try whenever you might need them! you can always come back to the book for a refresher.

some of these strategies are perhaps ones you already use or have considered trying and now, seeing them again, will be a reminder to you that it's time to ramp up your efforts in some way or to add a new tool or new strategy to the work you are already doing to get unstuck.

this book is like a *choose your own adventure* in that you get to pick and choose from the strategies that you need now and that will work for you... but it is also an invitation to go on a new adventure! to try something you haven't before... to see things in a new way... to take more consistent action with the stuck stuff in your life.

my wish is for you to feel empowered.

to go beyond the awareness of whatever has you feeling stuck, into a space of feeing empowered to actually *do something* about it.

to take yourself by the hand, and pull yourself up out of your stuckness.

to do the work to clear your foggy windows so that your light can shine a little brighter.

to RISE up out of the darkness and into the light.

`practice self-leadership.`

at the core, this book is about *self-leadership*: being a leader to yourself.

you might also think of it as *sovereignty*: taking dominion over yourself.

or you might connect to this idea when you remember: *my happiness depends on me. you all are off the hook.*

one of the reasons i love to use the word *revolution* in my work is because it is time to follow a new leader, one who will take you towards the future that you want for yourself. that leader is you.

here is my take on what self-leadership is all about...

self-awareness. know yourself. know your strengths, your dreams, your purpose. know what lights you up and fills your tank. know where you are going, who you are being, and why.

self-expression. own your voice. speak up for yourself. allow your true self to be seen. be authentic and vulnerable and real. expand your comfort zone.

self-direction. make choices that align with you. give yourself permission to do it your way, to do what serves you best. decide what matters.

self-motivation. back yourself. take action. do the work. take steps to get to where you want to be. pave your own path. alter your path!

self-responsibility. for where you are at. for building yourself up. for changing things. for your feelings. for healing. for your journey.

self-management. seek support when you need it. stay grounded in the here and now. come back to your path when you get off track.

self-guidance. connect to your inner self, your inner knowing, your inner guidance system. believe that you are exactly where you are meant to be, that this is your next step.

self-love. you are deserving and worthy of a beautiful life. you are enough as you are. you are here to shine... your light matters.

self-esteem, self-worth, self-confidence, self-fulfilment, self-belief, self-empowerment, self-transformation, self-trust, self-compassion, self-validation, self-determination, self-empowerment, self-transformation...

basically... take any word that describes what you want, need, or crave... and then put the word *self* in front of it and then remember that **your next step depends on you.**

i want you to have the tools to take that step... i want you to have the HOW... i want you to feel empowered in your own life... to have the strategies you need to take yourself by the hand, to pull yourself out of the muddy puddle you've been stuck in, to take steps forward towards more of what you say you want... to RISE and SHINE however you choose.

because the truth of it is this: change starts with you.

it's an inside job.

you cannot change anyone else around you – anyone that contributes to your stuckness – it is up to that person to change. **you can only change you.**

and no one else will come along and do this work for you... no one else is going show up and wave their magic wand and voila, things are different! **only you can change you.**

that might feel a little scary, a little hard. if you have been holding out for a hero to come along and slay your dragons or break you out of your prison box then recognising that YOU are the hero you have been waiting for might be a shock.

i will be very honest: getting unstuck is hard, y'all. truly. it's something i still work at every single day. there is one mantra i use over and over in my daily life, thanks to author glennon doyle[1]. i want you to practice it too:

we can do hard things.

in other words... you've got this!

are you ready to create a shift in your life? to clear the fog from your windows and shine a little brighter? to get unstuck and move forward? to RISE?

let's get started!

we *RISE* when we take responsibility.

part one:
awareness strategies

rise. 34

tools of awareness.

the first tool we have in our toolbelt for getting unstuck is awareness.

we RISE when we notice what stands in our way.

this might sound a little obvious... we need to know WHAT is actually in the way of us rising up and shining our light in order to clear it out or shift it in some way. but awareness can be tricky.

sometimes we don't *really* want to explore our stuckness... sometimes it simply feels too hard, too scary, or too insurmountable to face... sometimes we would rather avoid it, brush it under the carpet, pretend it doesn't exist, or just hope that it will go away by itself!

but the truth is, whatever obstacle we face — resistance, fear, worry, doubt, frustration, whatever — it won't go away by itself.

and, it is here for a reason.

acceptance.

having an acceptance that the obstacles are simply part of the journey can make them a lot easier to face. i believe they come up in our lives, and they come up WHEN they do, for a reason!

we are *supposed* to deal with them. they *are* our next step!

we can choose to see our resistance as something **blocking our way forward** or we can choose to see the resistance as a signpost pointing us in the **direction we need to go next**. that point of view is up to us!

note that this 'stuff' – resistance, fear, doubt, etc. – doesn't come up when we are doing things that don't really matter much. there are tasks we do, decisions we make, things we try every single day, every week and month, without ever feeling stuck. it's *no big deal.*

but the big stuff – the stuff that matters, the stuff that calls to us, the stuff that pushes us out of our comfort zone, the stuff that allows us to play bigger or do more or be more, the stuff that creates changes in our safe, same, small lives – *that's* where we are going to feel stuck.

the fear and doubt and worry and frustration comes up because *it matters.* and because it matters we need to accept that it's part of our job to face it all.

acceptance really changes the energy around the work we need to do to get unstuck and clear the fog... it is not 'hard work', it's not taking us away from our 'real work', it *is* the work.

willingness.

another thing that helps is having a willingness to shine a light on your stuckness and see what there is to see... to illuminate it with your awareness.

stuckness grows stickier the more we stay in the stuck place. the obstacles begin to feel larger and more difficult to move... the layers of fog just build and build. fear, worry, doubt... it all grows in the darkness.

a willingness to be aware and to explore and to do the work is the key.

notice.

what does the stuckness feel like to you right now? notice how you are responding or behaving.

- → **procrastination** - putting it off, delaying tactics, dragging heels
- → **avoidance** - sweep it under the rug, put your head in the sand
- → **excuses** - yah but... i know but... ok but...
- → **playing the victim** - blaming others, maintaining: 'it's not my fault'
- → **hitting a wall or ceiling** - feeling blocked, like something is holding you back

these experiences all point to something that you need to work on so that you can indeed make forward progress, so that you can do the things you say you want to do!

it's time to shine that light of awareness onto your stuckness and see what there is to see. you can't work on clearing it if you don't know what it is that is getting in your way!

the strategies in this section of the book will all help with awareness... but do be aware that there is more to this work than simply stating what you see, simply knowing what your stuckness is.

we also need to explore and seek understanding... we need to peel away the layers and look at what's happening at the core of the matter... we need to seek new perspectives or look at things with fresh eyes or from a different angle. and we need to be open to what we learn with new levels of awareness.

`spiral.`

here is a great way to think about it: we need to spiral with our stuckness.

if you picture a spiral in your mind it will remind you that you are not just spinning in circles, you are getting closer and closer to the centre, the core. a spiral also looks a bit like a cut onion... reminds us that there are layers to peel away, to look at what is going on deeper than the obvious!

if you think of the spiral as a staircase it reminds you that you can step away from the stuckness... you can look at it from above or below and get a new perspective. it is also a reminder that you can indeed take steps. if you are stuck in one spot on your staircase, on your journey, you can make the choice to stay stuck there or you can choose to take even one small step.

the staircase reminds us to check where we are at. we can be on the upward spiral... we can have a willingness to face the stuckness and take the steps and do the work. or we can be on the downward spiral with our excuses and victimhood and avoidance... believing that all of this is just too hard or too scary to deal with.

we RISE when we choose the upward spiral.

later in the book we will have some specific strategies for dealing with the various kinds of stuckness we face in life. those strategies at the core are about moving from the downward spiral into the upward spiral... changing not just our energy and our emotions but our actions and our words and our surroundings as well.

but for now, know that there is a simple way to get yourself out of that downward spiral of despair, frustration — the 'why bother' and the 'it's all too hard'...

play.

tap into the feelings of: joy. fun. wonder. curiosity. gratitude. pleasure. excitement. interest. exploration. adventure.

an attitude of playfulness and fun is the number one way to change your energy around the stuckness you face.

as you read this book, as you begin to have more awareness of whatever is causing your stuckness or fogging up your windows, try using playful, curious phrases like:

- hmmmmmm. i wonder why this is coming up?
- hmmmmmm. i wonder what i am here to learn?
- oh WOW! this is fascinating!
- ok, we are going in. let's do this.
- oh cool! this must be coming up for a reason!
- thank you for showing me what i need to work on!
- bingo! i see you there! gotcha!!

explore.

remember it's not enough to just recognize that you are stuck... we need tools to really explore the stuckness... to "go all in" with your light of awareness and your attitude of curiosity and see what there is to see.

part of our job here is to **connect the dots** between the things that we do notice and experience and explore. the core of our stuckness isn't always obvious and there are usually many different layers involved. often times the same things will come up again and again in new ways!

so not only do you need to have a willingness to explore you also need to be a bit of a seeker. think of yourself like a detective or a puzzle builder or even a pirate looking for treasure... you need to connect the dots between the pieces you uncover!

as we do the work to get unstuck and clear the fog we often go straight to the obvious. we might say something like: *"i have no confidence. i need to build up my confidence!"* and then we focus directly on a helpful confidence building strategy like practicing and practicing until we feel more confident.

makes sense, doesn't it? but the reason why many 'helpful strategies' don't really work in the long term is that they don't address the different layers of the issue, of the stuckness. this is why we must become dot connectors!

we need to explore all sorts of places to uncover anything that is adding to the stuckness or the fog. places like:

- **memories** associated with the issue
- **patterns** we are repeating
- **stories** we tell ourselves or others tell us
- **beliefs** that we carry with us
- **thoughts** that constantly run through our head
- **feelings** & emotions
- **behaviours** & actions
- **personality** traits & natural tendencies
- **values** that have been passed onto us
- **culture** of home, workplace, niche, community

you might even add to this list as you go! the point is to explore the underlying stuff behind the *obvious* stuckness because that is often where the real magic of clearing and shifting and change comes!

try.

here are some tools that may be handy on this journey of awareness, exploration, and dot connecting! some may already be 'go to' tools in your toolbelt, some may be new!

i encourage you to consider ramping up your efforts with your 'go to' favourite tools... be even more intentional with them, more consistent, or more curious! i also encourage you to perhaps try one new tool... you never know, it just might be the thing that adds a new layer to your inner work!

→ **journal**

there is incredible power in writing words to a page, with paper and pen. writing allows you to get whatever is going on *inside* of you *out of you*, by putting it down on the page. it also allows you to dig deeper, explore further, ask questions of yourself, connect the dots in new ways.

try: free writing. don't pause to think, to filter, to edit, to censor... just grab the pen and let the words flow.

→ **talk**

there is also incredible power in saying the words out loud. when we keep our stuckness hidden inside – unspoken, unseen – it grows in power. speaking out loud about whatever we are experiencing allows us to own it and become free to explore it... it also can release a big burden that comes from carrying things alone.

try: talking to a counsellor, therapist, mentor, or coach. talk to your friends or to a mastermind group. even talking out loud to yourself in the shower or the car can be powerful!

→ **oracle cards**

sometimes, when we only use our eyes and our brains to shine a light on our stuckness, we can miss things because we assume that what we see is *all* there is to see. oracle cards can point to new information that we perhaps hadn't considered or noticed!

try: as you are exploring your stuff pull a card and notice your first thought when you see/read the card. go with your own instinct... what it means to you IS what it means.

→ **signs & messages**

often when we start spiralling with our stuff we start to notice related information all around us. this is not a co-incidence! you've opened up the doorway for awareness, so make note of what you see. if a song comes on that catches your attention – what message does it have for you? if you notice a certain animal appearing over and over again – what message does it have for you?

try: keep a little notebook with you to keep track of the signs and messages you receive. if you notice it, if it brings up a meaning, it has meaning... to you! keeping track can help you identify patterns and messages, as well as strengthening the connection to this type of awareness.

→ **movement**

sometimes as we are doing this inner work of awareness and clearing we can actually get quite stuck in our heads and stuck in the spiral. in order to peel away new layers of awareness – to create flow for new levels of awareness to emerge – a change of pace or a change of scenery can make a big difference.

try: go for a long walk somewhere that inspires you; go out for a run and 'pound the pavement'; jump on a trampoline; go for a swim or a float; have a long bath or a long shower; go for a long car ride and sing out loud to the music on the radio; do a yoga class.

→ **meditation**

this is another way of getting out of your head... this time it's about getting into your soul! for me, meditation isn't about clearing all thoughts for total quiet, rather it's about clearing out the surface, mundane stuff so that there is room for the juicy stuff to come in! as you meditate, practice noticing – what pops into your head, what is your body telling you, what is your heart, your soul, your intuition, or your gut telling you?

try: a guided meditation, a kundalini meditation, a walking meditation, or a mindfulness meditation. one style of meditation might feel better to you than another!

these tools of awareness can be used at any time, for anything you are exploring... keep adding to these lists and keep practicing with the tools that work best for you.

to recap: remember your tools of awareness – acceptance, willingness, explore, play, connect dots, and spiral. next up, let's learn some awareness strategies that you can call upon no matter what stuckness you are experiencing!

***

play more: to explore the use of oracle cards as a tool for awareness, check out the illuminate oracle deck - karengunton.com/lho - there are many free resources there to help you get started.

do you have your own strategies, tools, and tips for awareness? do share them with us using the hashtag #iamariser... we can always add new ideas to our toolbox!

meet the lighthouse keepers.

my mission is to help people shine their light in the world... to BE a lighthouse in their own world in any way they choose. the lighthouse is much more than a metaphor meant to inspire you! it is actually a practical framework we can use to do the work.

the lighthouse consists of 7 components:

- the inner light
- the beacon
- the tower
- the foundation
- the spiral staircase
- the harbour
- the sky above

each of these components is needed but we often have some parts that are naturally stronger than others. some parts can become neglected or a bit wobbly over time, and some just need a little bit of attention!

the framework can offer us a valuable strategy for awareness no matter what sort of stuckness we are dealing with. we can go through each component, with our 'stuck stuff' in mind, and do a little exploring to see what we see.

my favourite way to explore my own lighthouse is to visualise each component being cared for by a particular lighthouse keeper – a personification or archetype that embodies each part of the lighthouse.

so let's take a guided journey through the lighthouse and meet each of the keepers – let's learn how each of them can help us to have more awareness of what we need to do in order to RISE... rise up tall like the lighthouse we are.

the following is a guided journey to meet the lighthouse keepers... and you can use this exercise whenever you would like to explore the components of your lighthouse

try using essential oils to support your intention to meet your lighthouse keepers: clary sage is the oil of clarity, and can help you with perspective, imagination, and vision.

note: the following guided journey is available as a recording that you can listen to – grab it at karengunton.com/free. or simply read through it now and visualise as you go. you might want to have a notebook handy to jot down anything that comes up!

before we begin, take a moment to feel grounded and centred. take a moment to open up your willingness and your awareness to this experience. open up to knowing, seeing, hearing, feeling, being with whatever comes... open up to receiving.

plant your feet firmly on the ground, feel the earth below you supporting you. wherever you are, sit (or stand) tall, aligned, with your back upright and your shoulders strong and your head held high.

picture yourself now as a lighthouse... rising up, standing tall, lighting up, and shining bright.

you have a light within you... as you take a deep breath in, picture that breath fanning the flames of your light. as you breathe in and out... put your hand on your brow, your third eye chakra, to help you notice the presence of our first lighthouse keeper... the visionary, the keeper of the inner light.

the visionary will help you tune into the **inner light** of your lighthouse — the light of your soul - and to check in with your *sight*: your perspective, focus, vision.

visionary asks: what do i see? what is happening or unfolding in front of me? what do i notice about me? what is my intuition showing me? do i feel excited, purposeful, ignited, clear?

when you are ready, take another deep breath and picture your light expanding outwards... beaming out like a guiding light. as you breathe in and out... put your hand on your neck, your throat chakra, to help you notice the presence of the next lighthouse keeper... the rockstar, the keeper of the beacon.

the rockstar will help you tune into the **beacon** of your lighthouse, the light you beam outwards — to check in with your *voice*: your words, your communication, what you hear.

rockstar asks: what do i say about this? what am i sharing with others? what am i hearing from others? do i feel authentic, genuine, vulnerable? am i seen, heard? am i able to push out of my comfort zone?

ok, take another deep breath and picture your light flooding into your heart. as you breathe in and out... put your hand on your chest, your heart chakra, to help you notice the presence of the next lighthouse keeper... the architect, the keeper of the tower.

the architect will help you to connect with the **tower** of your lighthouse — the vehicle that helps you to shine your light — and to check in with your *surroundings*: your physical stuff, your to do lists, your plans, your time.

architect asks: how is this working out for me? does this serve me? does it feel like me? do i love this? am i giving myself permission to do it my way? is this how i want to spend my time, energy, focus?

now, take another deep breath and picture your light moving downwards into your core. as you breathe in and out... put your hand on your stomach, your solar plexus chakra, to help you notice the presence of the next lighthouse keeper... the warrior, the keeper of the foundation.

the warrior will help you connect with the **foundation** of your lighthouse – that solid strength within you – to check in with your *action and mindset*.

warrior asks: can i do this? am i taking action? am i backing myself? do i stand up and fight for this? do i feel confident, courageous, resilient, worthy?

great, take another deep breath and picture your light spiralling, around and around, through your body. as you breathe in and out... put your hand low on your belly, your sacral chakra, to help you notice the presence of the next lighthouse keeper... the free spirit, the keeper of the spiral staircase.

the free spirit will help you to tune into the **spiral staircase** of your lighthouse – the journey you are on – to check in with your *emotions*: your feelings, your flow, your approach, and the journey so far.

free spirit asks: how do i feel? high vibe: curious, excited, creative, explore? low vibe: fear, worries, doubts, lack, stuck? am i willing to explore my feelings? am i willing to change my energy around this or change my approach?

when you are ready, take another deep breath and picture your light moving down through the bottom of your feet and into the earth. as you breathe in and out... put your hand at the base of your spine, your base chakra, to help you notice the presence of the next lighthouse keeper... the earth mama, the keeper of the harbour.

the earth mama helps us connect into the **harbour** of our lighthouse – the place where our lighthouse stands - to check in with your *space*: your presence, your BE-ing here in this moment

earth mama (or earth papa if you prefer) asks: am i here in the present (or stuck in past & future)? do i feel safe, supported, grounded, belonging, balanced? what am i allowing? what is my anchor? what is my 'come back rate' like when knocked off track?

last one, take another deep breath and picture a light shining down on you from the sky. as you breathe in and out... put your hand on the top of your head, your crown chakra, to help you notice the presence of our final lighthouse keeper... the sage, the keeper of the sky.

the sage helps you connect to the **sky** above your lighthouse – the source of your light – and check in with your *thoughts and beliefs*: your connection, your spirituality, your faith & trust

sage asks: do i believe i am where i am meant to be? do i believe universe has my back? do i know i am part of something bigger than me? do i have any signs & messages guiding me? do i feel connected to source?

take a final breath in to once again stand tall like a lighthouse and with a deep breath out let go of anything that no longer serves your light.

thank your lighthouse keepers for helping you to shine a light of awareness into each component of your lighthouse... thank them for helping you learn what you need in order to RISE... and remember that you can tune into each of these keepers whenever you need their help.

did your keepers have any insight to share with you? perhaps:

→ anything that might need to be ignited in some way or built in because it's not there right now;
→ anything that might need to be aligned or tweaked or adjusted so that it is a better fit for you;
→ anything that might need to be strengthened or cemented in because it serves you well;
→ and anything that may need to be cleared out, decluttered, shifted, released, or healed because it's not really serving you well!

the more you practice checking in with the 7 components of your own lighthouse the more awareness you will begin to have about whatever has you stuck.

sometimes when i am feeling stuck i will grab my notebook and use this visualisation to check in with each of my lighthouse keepers; i will ask each of them: *what do you need? what will help you to shine?* and then i will make a list... these are my **squad goals.**

for instance; as i noticed how much i was procrastinating in finishing this book my squad goals became:

- book in for a fresh new hair cut (my rockstar was feeling very blah and needed a boost to feel awesome and ready to shine)
- design and print a beautiful new year planner (my architect needed to make the book a priority and start planning and scheduling)
- reconnect to my why (my visionary needed a clear picture for what this book needed to be)
- remember i have done this before, i've got this! (my warrior needed a boost in confidence and strength)

making a list of my 'squad goals' helps me to think about ALL areas of my self and my life (not just one area that feels most pressing!) and it is such a great way to tune into and honour my self... each of these lighthouse keepers lives within me already, so by exploring what each of them is longing for or dreaming of or wanting more of in life i am actually taking beautiful care of my self!

if you notice worry, doubt, fear, frustration, or lack – or maybe you notice that you are procrastinating, you feel lost, you have no mojo, you are avoiding –

or you notice any other kind of stuckness... try checking in with your squad – your lighthouse keepers – they are always there within you, ready to help you shine.

***

play more: for more on the 7 lighthouse keepers and how you can strengthen, activate, and explore each component of your lighthouse grab the free 'lighthouse keepers' digital magazine at karengunton.com/free

meet your shadow hunter.

the stuckness — the darkness, the shadows, the storms — it's important to acknowledge that this stuff is indeed simply part of the journey we are on... because it's the other side of the light.

i know i talk about being a lighthouse... being our highest, brightest selves so that we can shine. but the light is not the whole story... of course. you wouldn't be reading this book if you didn't feel stuck in the darkness in some way!

so how do we explore this stuckness? we can become a shadow hunter, we can peer into the darkness, and we can shine a light on whatever it is that we are meant to face, explore, or heal now.

when i am feeling stuck, i like the idea of firmly planting my two feet on the ground, facing the darkness head on, as if it is a cave, and proclaiming: "ok! i'm going in!" it creates playfulness, a sense of curiosity and adventure... rather than seeing this as something hard, scary, or avoided.

and i don't think we need to be shadow 'fixers' or shadow 'conquerors'.... i don't think that's the point.

facing the darkness doesn't mean we are broken... it's not about fixing it.

it's about facing it. knowing it. owning it. embracing it.

perhaps in facing the darkness we will find our light.

in feeling our pain we will experience healing. in knowing our fear we will discover courage. in understanding our shame we will cultivate compassion... for ourselves. in recognizing our biggest challenge we will uncover our greatest gift. in meeting our demons we will be able to let them go... so they no longer hold the same power over us.

maybe, by owning the shadow side of ourselves — the stuff about us that we aren't so good at, or proud of, or that we try to hide away — we will stop feeling *less than* because of it.

for no one is perfect. no one is all light, all the time. and placing that impossible expectation upon ourselves will always make us feel, in some way or another, like we are not enough.

maybe when we embrace our own shadows we will see that we are still worthy... worthy of love and joy and abundance and success and all of it.

maybe exploring our darkness is about deciding to just BE where we are, here and now. to stop avoiding, running, or hiding from the darkness... to stop pretending it isn't there... but instead to set up camp inside of it, to decide: this is a part of me and i will build up from this place.

but HOW?

how do we explore our darkness? how do we confront our shadows? how do we face our biggest storms, and come out the other side to shine our light?

let's go on another journey, the one to meet your inner shadow hunter.

try using essential oils to support your intention of meeting your shadow self – juniper berry is the oil of the night and can help with facing the shadows and the darkness.

note: the following guided journey is available as a recording that you can listen to – grab it at karengunton.com/free. or simply read through it now and visualise as you go. you might want to have a notebook handy to jot down anything that comes up!

before we begin, take a moment to feel grounded and centred. take a moment to open up your willingness and your awareness to this experience. open up to knowing, seeing, hearing, feeling, being with whatever comes... open up to receiving.

put your hand on your heart or over your solar plexus/upper stomach – or perhaps another spot calls to you as the spot inside of you where your shadows are hiding. put your hand there now and take a deep breath in and a deep breath out.

say out loud: *arms wide open, i am ready, it is safe to go on this journey to meet my shadow hunter.*

picture yourself inside a beautiful lighthouse. you are up at the very top, right there with the beautiful light... the inner light that burns bright and gentle from within. picture this light in your mind and know that you are safe here, for this light is the light of your soul. feel it envelope you in a warm embrace.

when you are ready, it's time to descend the spiral staircase within the centre of the lighthouse, one step at a time, down, down, down. the journey is easy, yet you may begin to feel a bit uncomfortable the further down you go, below the surface, into the darkness, away from the light.

take a deep breath in and as you breathe out imagine that breath releasing any worry, fear, or discomfort you feel.

remember that your shadow hunter is strong and brave... playful and kind... they wouldn't call you to meet them in the shadows if it wasn't safe to do so. trust in that and let yourself feel excited about what you might find.

as you descend down, step by step, further into the darkness notice when you feel that strong, brave presence arrive next to you. reach out your hand knowing that your shadow hunter will find it, and grasp it, with strength and assurance. feel them there with you, beside you, taking the lead.

walk through the darkness with your shadow hunter. though you can't see anything yet, allow yourself to be drawn to a certain place in the darkness, a certain room deep down in the furthest reaches... you know this room is the one you need to explore. go towards that room now, and trust that you aren't alone. your shadow hunter is there, brave and adventurous, ready to lead the way.

notice how you feel as you approach the room in the darkness. what are the feelings and thoughts that bubble up as you consider the demons that are waiting within? do you notice fear, unworthiness, shame, uncertainty, criticism, judgement? what are the whispers coming from behind the door... what words pop into your head?

take a moment now to recognize the feelings, words, thoughts, beliefs, etc. that are coming up as you get ready to walk into this particular room. whatever is popping up may be uncomfortable, perhaps you have a sensation that you should turn back, walk away from this uncomfortable darkness, back into the light.

again, take a deep breath, feel the presence of your brave shadow hunter there with you, and know it is safe to experience whatever is coming up for you now.

squeeze your shadow hunter's hand, this is your signal that you are ready to go into that dark room and see what there is to see. as you open the doorway and step inside, your shadow hunter lights a candle. it emits a gentle, golden light. it's not harsh on your eyes, it's warm and comforting. you feel it envelope you, and the darkness no longer feels so uncomfortable.

you feel confident now and take the candle from your shadow hunter. you direct the beam of light into each of the corners of the room. now is your chance to illuminate the darkness... do so with a sense of curiosity.

ask out loud: *what do i need to see? what am i here to learn?*

and notice. what does this room represent to you about your own shadow self, your dark side, or the demons you've been perhaps avoiding?

what have you been keeping hidden away in this room? are there memories? old stories? baggage that you've been carrying around with you? the voices of your inner critic, your inner imposter, your inner demons... your shame or hurt or pain? a part of yourself that you'd rather not embrace?

now is the time to explore. you are safe. and you are supported. your shadow hunter stands beside you, emitting the vibes of confidence, curiosity, playfulness even. you have a strong sense that nothing in this room is actually as bad as it ever seemed!

you notice that the longer you stay in the room, the illuminating light of the candle grows brighter and brighter and you feel even more comfortable... you know that the stuff that has been hidden away in this room has no power over you in the light! and you trust that all this room has for you now is helpful information. take as much time as you need to explore.

when you are ready, squeeze the hand of your shadow hunter again... it's time to go. this time, as you walk away from the room, you close the door but the light remains. you've embraced these shadows, there will be no more festering in the darkness. you close the door as a symbol that you have taken what you needed to learn and you've left the rest behind. it no longer holds the power of fear, doubt, worry, lack, or frustration over you.

you walk away confident, and settled, even excited because your journey into the darkness provided you with some helpful insight! your shadow hunter leads you back to your spiral staircase... as you prepare to ascend once again they give you a big hug. and they whisper a message in your ear...

i am always here. i am the brave, bold, curious, adventurous part of your soul... ready to explore the shadows. i am the ying to the yang of your ignited, brightest self... and absolutely as important to the journey.

whenever you need to explore the darkness, call on me. i am the shadow hunter, and with me **you are safe to be all that you are... both the light and the dark.**

meet your inner child.

a journey to meet your inner child can be an interesting way to explore and uncover some of the underlying layers of your stuckness. your inner child may help point to some of those thoughts, beliefs, memories, stories, patterns, behaviours, personality traits, etc that add up to whatever is going on for you right now.

it might seem like a 'too simple' or even 'silly' thing to do – asking your inner child what they have to say about your stuck stuff! but really, when was the last time you thought about the inner child inside of you? one that may have been deeply hurt by actions of the past... one that may be feeling the fear, worry, doubt intensely... one who might have hopes and dreams unrecognized!

the following is a guided journey to meet your inner child... and you can use this exercise whenever you would like to explore the layers of your stuckness in a new way, with a new perspective.

try using essential oils to support your intention to meet your inner child – ylang ylang is the oil of the inner child; it will help you feel free, joyful, and connected to what's in your heart.

note: the following guided journey is available as a recording that you can listen to – grab it at karengunton.com/free. or simply read through it *now and visualise as you go. you might want to have a notebook handy to jot down anything that comes up!*

before we begin, take a moment to feel grounded and centred. take a moment to open up your willingness and your awareness to this experience. open up to knowing, seeing, hearing, feeling, being with whatever comes... open up to receiving.

put your hand on your lower belly or on your heart or perhaps another spot calls to you as the spot inside of you where your inner child has been waiting. put your hand there now and take a deep breath in and a deep breath out.

say out loud: *arms wide open, i am ready, it is safe to go on this journey to meet my inner child.*

picture yourself inside a beautiful lighthouse. you are up at the very top, right there with the beautiful light... the inner light that burns bright and gentle from within. picture this light in your mind and know that you are safe here, for this light is the light of your soul. feel it envelope you in a warm embrace.

when you are ready, it's time to descend the spiral staircase within the centre of the lighthouse. take a step down and then another, down and around you go, down the spiral staircase. the journey is easy, and you are looking forward to meeting your inner child.

you come to the front door of your lighthouse... open it up and step through. pause for a moment...

what do you see in front of you as you emerge? this is the place your inner child feels safe and happy, and it is indeed safe for you to walk outside.

notice where you are: a room? an outside space? a pathway?

notice what you see: are there any physical objects? colours? symbols?

notice how you feel: do you feel any emotions? what do you feel in your body?

notice anything else: a word pops in your head? music?

whatever you notice, trust it! your inner child has chosen this just for you. take a gentle breath in and begin to walk away from the front door. walk ahead with a willingness to explore.

as you walk along, notice when your inner child arrives to walk beside you. reach out, allow them to hold your hand.

what do you notice about them: appearance, emotions, actions, words, or energy?

take a moment just to be with them, to walk beside them, to feel their presence.

when you are ready you might want to ask them a question. for instance ask: what would you like me to know? (or perhaps what would you like me to see, say, do, feel, believe, be?)

listen to what they have to tell you. and then consider, is there anything you would like to tell them? what do you want them to know now?

have a chat. offer a hug. cry or laugh perhaps. spend as much time with your inner child as you like.

when you are ready, walk together back to your lighthouse, hand in hand. open the door and walk back up the spiral staircase. the journey is still easy, and in fact feels even lighter before. notice the joy in your heart.

with each step you take... as you get closer and closer to the top, and closer and closer to the centre of the light... remember that your inner child is there with you now. you can spend time with them again whenever you wish.

they are there within the light of your soul.

meet your future self.

just like your inner child may have some helpful insight for you, your future self also has a very important perspective!

often times we feel the most stuck — the most fear, doubt, worry, and frustration — when we are taking steps towards something important in our lives... when we are RISING up in some way:

- upleveling.
- stepping up.
- playing big.
- being seen.
- speaking out.
- taking action.
- stepping forward.
- showing up in a bigger way with your life or your work.
- shining your light even brighter.

when i talk to people about building a lighthouse or BEing the lighthouse, i remind them that this simply means: **to be the highest, brightest, best version of you**... "lighthouse you."

let's just think about that for a moment.

a you that is confident, feels worthy, implicitly believes in yourself.

a you that is completely authentic, bold, and brave.

a you that is not afraid, knows you are not going to fail, trusts that you do make a difference.

successful, famous, rich you. thought leader, trailblazer, revolutionary you. steady, grounded, fulfilled you.

the you that is the leader. the teacher. the explorer. the connector. the healer. the transformer. the storyteller. the creator.

inspirational, creative, courageous, vulnerable, soulful, strong, grounded, guided, empowered, happy, productive, balanced, ignited you.

in this guided journey we are going to meet future you... lighthouse you... the you that has done it: has risen, stands tall, is lit up from within, and shines bright.

try using essential oils to support your intention to not just meet future you but to *embody* future you – rosemary is the oil of knowing, it will help you to feel inspired and to feel confident in this new perspective.

note: the following guided journey is available as a recording that you can listen to – grab it at karengunton.com/free. or simply read through it now and visualise as you go. you might want to have a notebook handy to jot down anything that comes up!

before we begin, take a moment to feel grounded and centred. take a moment to open up your willingness and your awareness to this experience. open up to knowing, seeing, hearing, feeling, being with whatever comes... open up to receiving.

put your hand on your heart or on your brow/third eye or perhaps another spot calls to you as the spot inside of you ready to connect with 'future you'. put your hand there now and take a deep breath in and a deep breath out.

say out loud: *arms wide open i am ready, it is safe to go on this journey to meet future me.*

picture yourself standing in a harbour. feel your feet in the sand, feel the sun on your face and the breeze in your hair. take a deep breath in of that beautiful fresh air. know that you are safe here, know that you are free to explore.

look out across the harbour, just across from where you stand. there, standing on the rocky cliff, is future you.

they are there standing tall, feet firmly planted on the earth, rising up, strong in stature... head held high, spine straight, shoulders back, hands and heart open wide.

you see the you of the future standing there across the harbour and your heart has a longing to go to out to them.

yet it may also feel like it is a long way to go. the journey may seem difficult at first – perhaps it is a big harbour to cross, perhaps fraught with crashing waves or debris left behind by the storms, perhaps there is a rock face that seems impossible to climb.

what do you see in front of you?

take a deep breath in and as you breathe out let that breath settle and calm everything around you. know that the only way forward is simply taking one step at a time... one foot in front of the other... left, right, left, right. you can do that, you can easily take one step at a time.

walk along the shoreline, closer and closer to future you... keep breathing, keep stepping, and know that you are safe. future you would never beckon you closer if it wasn't safe for you to cross the harbour.

as you get closer and closer, become more and more aware of future you.

what do they look like? what are they wearing? have they got any accessories or distinguishing features?

what is their energy like? who are they BEing? what are they doing? what is the space like where they stand? what energy or vibe are they giving out?

once you are standing right in front of future you, allow them to bring you into a warm embrace. soak up their whole vibe, allow it to surround you... this is the light of their soul.

give future you a name, a nickname, or a persona... let it be something meaningful to both of you, something you can use to call upon their presence and wisdom from now on. perhaps a name like "wise me" "inner mentor" "future me" "real me" "lighthouse me" ... or maybe a special nick name that has meaning to you or that evokes their powerful vibe.

once you know their name, sit down with them and have a chat. this is your opportunity to ask questions!

→ what would you like to know about them?
→ what are their relationships like?
→ what fun, adventure, travel have they done?
→ what have they created? achieved? accomplished?
→ what have they changed? what have they released or healed or cleared?
→ how do they define freedom, success, happiness?
→ and finally, what do they want you to know now?
→ what advice do they have for you?
→ what is the one thing they want you to know for sure?
→ what do they want you to remember, always?

one very important thing to remember is that future you is the highest, brightest version of you. the you that has done the work, the you that has risen up to stand tall and shine bright and achieve your dreams.

remember always as you travel along this journey and feel stuck, lost, afraid, uncertain, dejected, etc... you can always connect with future you by asking out loud...

what would *they* do? what would 'lighthouse me' or 'real me' do? make it an acronym to remember... WWLHD?

the answer is there.

and know this one thing for sure... you do not have to wait until you are suddenly, magically the you of the future. the time is now.

you can start practicing.

you can act as if.

you can embody that version of you. right now.

the one BIG challenge.

i have this theory.

i think that we each have one big thing to deal with in our lifetime... the big challenge we face, the big question we have to answer, the big obstacle we have to overcome, the big lesson we are here to learn, the big story we have been telling ourselves for a long time... that one big thing that shows up again and again in our lifetime for us to work through.

my big challenge is about enoughness. the bullshit story that seems to come up again and again in my head is: i am not enough. this is not enough. it's not unique, significant, smart, successful, special, worth enough. it's never going to land. the other side of that coin is a story about being too much: too weird, too bossy, or dangerously shining too bright. and just when i think i have cleared that block or changed that story, it sneaks back in again!

as i have been working on finishing this book, after the period of stuckness that i have been in for the past while, it almost feels like being back at square one again. the voice in my head says: *you are not enough. this is not enough. why bother? no one actually cares anymore. your time to shine is over.*

but then i remember that i am not in fact at square one. i have amassed so much evidence of my enoughness , and i have the tools i need to deal with that pesky voice! all of the work i have already done in my big challenge area is the foundation i build on now. yes, i got knocked down... but the platform i landed on is actually quite a bit stronger than it once was.

and that's the beauty of knowing your 'big challenge'. by acknowledging it, we can more easily recognize it when it comes up again and again... and with that awareness, the big challenge loses some of its power over us, some of its heavy weight.

it becomes just *that thing* we are here to do in this life time.

oh hey there BIG, persistent, challenging thing... i see that you're back again. ok then, let's do this. i am ready for you this time.

there is a great saying that describes this well: new level, new devil. although, in this case i think it would be fitting to say: **new level, same old devil.**

so how can you figure out what your one big challenge is?

here are some clues...

- that **poor me/victim** place that you go to when things get hard: *why does this always happen to me? why doesn't anybody ever...? when is it going to change? it's so unfair! wahhhhh.*

- that situation that seems to **push your buttons** every time, no matter how much you try to move past it: *omg, i cannot believe that he said that... he did that...he made me feel like...!!!*

- that **excuse** you come up with to stay where you are: *i want to, but... i would, except... i tried, but... that's great for you, but... but, my situation is special.*

- that **pattern** that you seem to play out over and over again: *this happens, and then i do this, and then that happens, and then i feel like...*

- the **sweeping generalisations** you make about your life: *of course that happened! the story of my life. it always goes that way. i never get to...*

- that **story** you were told or taught when you were little about who you are, what your job is, where you are going: *be good, don't rock the boat, stay small, don't disappoint, you can't, you're not*

these clues might make it seem like you have more than one big thing... but if you start to dig a little deeper, explore a little further, connect the dots, you might find that in the end they all are pieces of the same puzzle... the same big challenge.

it might be really hard to figure this out about yourself at first. when we are deep in the trenches of our stuff we don't always see the big picture created by all those little puzzle pieces.

but you can practice by becoming more aware of the people in your life... see if you can figure out what *their* one big thing is. (it's way easier to recognize this in other people because we aren't so close to it, plus i think we are more naturally inclined to want help others rather than figure out how to help ourselves.)

for instance, you might notice that someone in your life always seems to say: *no one ever listens to me anyways, no one ever seems to care what i have to say about it.* their big challenge might be around being seen and heard.

someone else in your life might seem to always find themselves in a pattern of people pleasing... maybe their one big thing to learn here is how to stand in their own truth, create boundaries, or put themselves first.

it's actually very helpful to recognize the big challenge for the important people in your life. not that you ought to *tell them* what you think they need to do or help them to navigate it, but rather because it helps *you* to see that we each are on our own journey and sometimes their stuff is indeed just *their stuff* – the stuff they are here to learn – and **it's not actually about you.**

it helps us to have compassion for others; even if we don't want to be in the trenches with them and their stuff we can still let them go from a place of compassion.

plus, the more you can catch those clues in the people around you, the more you can start to catch them for yourself too.

once your own one big challenge makes itself clear to you, what do you do?

awareness is the key, because with awareness, the energy around that big thing will begin to change. you will see yourself and your challenges a bit differently, plus you will be more willing to tackle this stuff head on when you know it's what you are here to do... you will approach your challenges in a new way.

try to **reframe** that big challenge or big question or big obstacle in a new way.

for example, with my big challenge of enoughness, i find myself often saying: *when will i be enough? when will it land for me?*

i try to catch myself now and reframe those questions into something more positive and helpful... i am enough, just as i am. it is enough, it is landing. i see evidence of my enoughness all of the time.

i also believe that our biggest challenge — our deepest wound, our lowest tide — is actually our greatest gift... for it is when the tide is at its lowest that we can find the treasures in the sand. and it is through our darkness that we find our light.

i started the lighthouse revolution, not because i had discovered what i was here to teach in this lifetime, but rather because it **was what i needed to learn myself.**

the lighthouse is what i needed in my own life and work to navigate my way through the darkness... i built exactly what would help me to clear my fog and RISE up and shine my light. my efforts to face my darkness head on have become the gift that i am here to share with others.

and so, if facing your one big thing is indeed what you are here to do in this lifetime, why not face it head on? tap into your inner free spirit, your inner playful explorer/adventurer, and face it head on with a sense of wonder, of curiosity... ready to spiral with your stuff... to learn and grow... knowing that with each little step you take you've taken one step closer to your light.

what is your one big challenge for this lifetime?

the swinging pendulum.

i have another theory. like the one big challenge, i think we each experience periods of extremes in our lifetime, and these extremes are here to help us find our **natural sweet spot** – the balance that works best for us.

i think of this like a swinging pendulum between two opposites.

that image might already bring something to mind: a swing that you can tell you have been on between one extreme and its opposite in some area of your work or your life, or perhaps a swing that you have never been able to truly find your happy medium on.

back at the start of 2018 i chose 'magnetic' as my word for the year, and i remember as i set that intention i felt more in tune, clear, guided, and connected than i ever had before... it was like i started the year on freaking fire. i felt like my power was turned on, with validation, inspiration, and confirmation coming in like crazy... i felt wide open, highly sensitive, truly magnetic. it just so happened that i was also attracting a bunch of stuff i needed to heal, face, work on... every one of my buttons seemed to be getting pushed all at once.

i suppose that getting super clear, feeling guided, and taking inspired action also brought up lots of doubt, worry, and fear. it makes sense to me now, but back then all of that combined with a big dose of loss and grief... it was a lot. and so i shut down my sensitivity and connection. it was as though i hung out a neon sign: *closed. do not disturb.*

just recently i received an invitation to join a workshop about spiritual connection and my instinct was: *no. nope. not ready to open up.* in that moment i became aware of my swinging pendulum — how i had gone from wide open ready to closed tight shut — and i believe that my fear about opening back up again is a clue for the exact thing i need to work on next.

perhaps you've been experiencing one of these pendulums:

- masculine vs feminine
- anxiety vs control
- strategy vs spontaneity
- doing vs being
- efforting vs flow
- pushing vs pulling
- trying vs allowing
- logic vs intuition
- hard work vs ease
- rigidity vs rebellion
- extroversion vs introversion
- closed off vs wide open
- practical vs purposeful
- action vs retreat
- active vs sedentary

- energised vs inertia
- bingeing vs deprivation

you could probably keep adding to this list! you might even choose different words that feel like a better fit for your own polar extremes.

of course we experience normal fluctuations in these areas of ourselves and our lives all of the time... that is life! what we are looking for in this particular awareness strategy is:

→ that one area that seems to really push your buttons,
→ that one big struggle for balance that you just can't seem to find,
→ or that one swinging pendulum that seems particularly extreme.

i think we experience this set of extremes for a reason: we must experience both sides of the coin in a big way or experience a big discomfort in our attempt to 'fit', in order to truly find our balance... to find the sweet spot where the magic happens.

and once we've experienced the extremes and the discomfort, once our pendulum stops swinging so wildly and settles into our sweet spot, we also have greater power and more awareness to know when it is best to work with one side of the coin or the other.

i also think that the swinging pendulum seems to happen when we find ourselves in a new situation.

perhaps we have a career change, or a change from being an employee to being self-employed, or a change from being busy taking care of others to having more time to take care of yourself, or the change that comes with a big move or a big loss, or a change in some other area of your life: health, relationships, finances, etc.

it is as though we have been in a certain box that has contained us for a long time and suddenly we are in a new situation, one with new freedom or maybe one with new expectations. we have to find a new way forward now and that sets the pendulum swinging.

perhaps we go from being incredibly busy to suddenly having more time, and then we just don't feel like doing anything at all! or perhaps we go from giving and people pleasing and poor boundaries to getting burned or burning out so you build big walls and you protect yourself away.

the thing about the swinging pendulum is that neither extreme is all that healthy or satisfying to be in the long term, but we must experience them both to learn from the discomfort. and then we must see the extremes as the opportunity... the gift... to find our sweet spot.

perhaps there is already a set of extremes that you can sense is your swinging pendulum... now is a good time to ask:

- → what do i need to learn and experience in each extreme?
- → what are the best parts and the worst parts of each, for me?
- → where do my strengths and weaknesses lie, in each?
- → what would life be like if i found the sweet spot?
- → how can i give myself permission to be in that sweet spot more often?

like with the big challenge, sometimes we don't see our own swinging pendulum that clearly. you can practice noticing it in yourself by recognizing it in others... in fact i bet someone's name has already popped into your head!

next time you do find yourself in an extreme consider: where or when has the opposite also been true for you? understanding the path that got you here can help you to find the right happy medium for you now.

the swinging pendulum can take place over an entire life time, or it can be something that is more sudden and immediate... either way there are layers of awareness for you in that experience.

as i think about my own swinging pendulum, i wonder: why did i shut down? that feeling of open magnetism was incredible but it also scared me... recognising my own power turned on scared me and there was also perhaps a fear of shining too bright, of being on the cusp of something possibly great.

the new middle i am seeking is one where i feel open AND safe: where i know that nothing will be sent my way that i cannot handle, where i have trust in myself and in the universe, and where i remember that i am the damn hero of my story... i can do hard things AND i can receive amazing things.

what do the extremes that you are experiencing have to show you?

we RISE when we find our sweet spot.

the wreck.

i have one more theory to share with you about life. this is a phenomenon that i have noticed as i have written and published my own books and have been watching and learning from other authors. at first, i named this phenomenon *writer's wreck* but i actually believe it is something ALL of us ought to be aware of, because i feel like it happens in more areas of life and work and self, than just when writing a book.

here is what i have seen happen over and over again: we experience a big "wreck" — a crash and burn, a rock bottom, a complete fail — with the very thing we are meant to be good at or that we are here to share with others.

the book topic you are writing about, the stuff you are teaching, the community you've started, the expertise you help others with, the thing you are most passionate about, the thing everyone says you are so good at... suddenly you yourself experience a big issue with that very thing.

- the author writing about love goes through a bad breakup of their marriage
- the expert teaching how to have a balanced life experiences a massive period of stress, overwhelm, and unbalance
- the spiritual mentor sharing a message that the universe has your back has a complete crisis of

faith and trust, feeling untethered and unsupported
- the friend who is always such a go-getter action taker has a period of depression and can't do much of anything
- the entrepreneur who has a mission to help people shine their light finds herself absolutely lost in the darkness

the wreck can feel like you've lost your mojo for the very thing you are passionate about; it can feel like you are a failure at the thing you are supposed to be good at; or it can feel like you've become a fraud because you can't manage it yourself... so how are you supposed to help others?

knowing that the wreck is actually a *thing people go through* – and i promise you they do! – can be quite comforting. you realize that it's not something that is *wrong* with you (you aren't a failure or a fraud) but rather it's just part of the journey we are on.

why is it part of the journey? why does it happen?

here's my theory...

we experience the wreck so that we know how it feels to be in the shoes of the people we are here to help, inspire, teach, or touch.

our capacity to find our way through to the other side – how we get unstuck, how we clean our foggy windows, how we shift the obstacles in our way — becomes what we can share with others.

in other words, **your wreck becomes your gift**... your darkness becomes the light you shine.

plus, the wreck occurs to force us to walk the talk, to practice what we preach, to use our own tools... perhaps in ways we haven't really had to yet. it is a sort of **upleveling**: *so, these are the tools you swear by? ok let's test them!*

once we see the wreck for what it is — an opportunity — we can become more compassionate with ourselves, gentle on ourselves.

we can be curious: hmmmm, i wonder why this is happening now? i wonder what i am meant to learn or experience?

we can be grateful for the opportunity to practice our own gifts.

we can be open to allowing even new gifts and skills and tools and capacity to emerge.

in other words, we can treat ourselves with the very intention that we hold for others.

this is the true gift of the wreck.

think about it. if you are here to help someone heal or learn or grow or play or explore or shine, in any way at all, how would you treat them? knowing how tricky life can be, what would you most want them to know?

the wreck is the opportunity not only to experience the very problem you long to solve but even more importantly, the opportunity to treat yourself with the compassion that you hold for others.

instead of berating yourself: how does an unstucktor get so damned stuck? how can a spiritual guide lose faith? how does a health coach end up in such an unhealthy state? what the hell is wrong with me?

remember: it is not the unstucktor who is stuck... it is the human. the unstucktor or spiritual guide or health coach is still there inside of you, observing from a distance... but human you must have this experience.

the next time you find yourself crashing and burning in some way, instead of judging yourself harshly, allow yourself to surrender to the wreck... let this rock bottom you experience become the foundation from which you can RISE... ask: *what would you have me do?*

when was the last time you checked in with the thing you were so sure about, so good at? the wreck knocks the foundation of your surety away... you get to unlearn, relearn, explore, practice. it's a gift.

you have seen my descent. now watch me RISE.

the road so far.

my favourite tv show is a show called <u>supernatural</u>[2], a show with 15 seasons: a lot of history, a lot of twists and turns, a whole lot has happened. each new season begins with an excellent recap called 'the road so far' always set to an epic, classic rock tune. *the road so far* recap is essential viewing even to the most obsessed fan because no matter how much you love the show, no matter how much you obsess over every detail, you still won't remember everything!

the road so far gives us the highlights, the recap, the important bits of everything that has happened before... we get reminded of the pieces of the puzzle that have brought us to this point in the story so that we can make sense of what comes next. plus, if you watch carefully, the road so far often offers a hint or clue as to how the heroes will solve the big dilemma in the story ahead.

many tv shows do this, it's not revolutionary. i just like that my show calls it *the road so far* and i think this is something we ourselves can use as an awareness strategy.

whatever stuckness you feel right now, that is the 'season' you are in in the story of your life. in order to jump in right now, to try to figure out what is happening, and also to make sense of where you are going, it can help to get caught up on those puzzle pieces from the past.

we need our own little recap of *the road so far*, we need to see the moments that have brought us here... we can look back at the past to make sense of where we are now, in this 'episode', and where we might be going next in the story.

just as if you were planning the recap for the tv show of your life, consider your current stuckness – your predicament, your struggle, your issue, or your pain – and have a look back at your own *road so far* to make note of some of those puzzle pieces.

look through your memories... recall people and places and situations... remember actions and reactions, successes and failures, choices and decisions... reflect on the bits that stand out as well as the bits that you'd rather forget.

try thinking of any AHA moments, turning points, forks in the road, sliding doors... those pivotal times that really shaped you and have brought you right here, to this moment in time.

this little exercise is not meant to put you in a place where you beat yourself up in any way over the past... this is simply about awareness.

as i was looking back through some of my old notebooks to find bits and pieces for this book i found a page with this phrase along with a big question mark: *you are a healer.*

a few years ago i attended a retreat, part of which was an opportunity to talk with an intuitive guide who was a voice channel sharing messages from our soul guides. their message for me was: *you are a healer.*

at the time i found that so confusing! i identified as a teacher, a creator, and possibly even a leader, but definitely not a healer. i helped people find their purpose, build their mindset, and shine their light in the world and i couldn't really see how what i did was 'healing'... hence the giant question mark on this old page of my notebook.

but now what i know for sure is that everything i have experienced, the journey i have been on, brought me here... to healing. which as we defined at the beginning of this book means coming back to your *self.*

now, looking back at my road so far, i have an AHA: i am a healer because i have what i need within me and around me to heal myself.

as you look back at your own road so far you might notice some patterns or recurring themes, some sign posts that make so much more sense with the 20/20 vision of hindsight, or even some valuable information about who you are and why you do what you do.

you also might notice some things that you need to release or forgive or clear or reframe in some way... there will be some great strategies for doing all of that in the next section.

looking back at *the road so far* can be a helpful way to connect the dots of your own story... it can be really hard to see the stuff we are in the middle of right now – it's so raw and complex and challenging – but you might find that time and distance and space will afford you all sorts of clarity when it comes to looking back at the journey that has brought you here.

we RISE when we look back to have a clearer picture of how to move forward.

one more thing we can learn from my show, supernatural: every script ends with **...to be continued...** and that is the beauty of this road you are on. you get to decide where you go next.

the destination dream.

just as it is important to be aware of where we are right now and where we have been to get us to this place, we also ought to be aware of where we are going next.

you are reading this book because you want to RISE. you want to get unstuck or remove the obstacles in your way and create a change in your life... you want to do more and have more and be more of whatever it is you say you want.

so what exactly does that look like for you? what is *your* version of RISING? what is the change that you want to create?

if we really want to make a change away from something 'old' it helps to have a clear idea of what exactly we are moving towards... this your **towards vision** or your **destination dream**. without that vision or that goal or that place we know we want to arrive, it can be pretty easy to let ourselves stay stuck.

sometimes it is difficult to know where we are going.

we may recognize that we aren't in a great place, we may wish for things to be different, we may feel deeply that life can be better than it is... but we may not be 100% sure what that actually looks like.

that's ok! even if you don't know what it looks like you might know how you want to feel or how you'd rather be spending your time. there is more than one way to create your destination dream!

you may also be tempted to say something like: *i am open to whatever life has in store for me!* or: *i don't like to have a goal or a vision, i prefer to go with the flow.* these non-committal answers are a sign of avoidance, it's the voice of your stuckness talking! it matters for you to **say and own what you want.**

one way to get awareness for where you want to go from here or what you are working towards is to let yourself dream of a time in the future when things are different for you.

ask yourself:

- who do i want to be?
- what do i want to do?
- how do i want to feel?
- what do i want to say?
- where do i want to go?
- what do i want to have?

glennon doyle, in her book <u>untamed</u> asks: *what is the truest most beautiful story about your life that you can imagine?*

use your answers to create a picture of what you are working towards... your destination. you might try:

- → describe your ideal day, ideal job, ideal relationship, or ideal situation
- → make a vision board to represent what you want
- → write a letter as though it is one year from now describing your life

some people find it quite easy to visualise a destination in their mind's eye but for others this may not work well.

i am not great at 'visualising' as in seeing a picture in my head. you will note i called the strategies on meeting your shadow hunter etc. 'guided journeys' rather than 'guided visualisations' ...my brain just doesn't work that way!

you might find that words, stories, quotes, phrases, even music lyrics will help to create a 'picture' of your destination. or perhaps for you it is more of a deep knowing, a feeling in your core or a sensation in your body, which lets you know you've hit on what you want. you might need to talk or write or sketch or physically create something in order to create the picture of your destination.

play, explore, and do what works for you!

an important note here – this is not about making a plan, or figuring out all of the directions and steps and pathways that will get you where you want to go. this is not a *'how to'*. this simply about the *where*.

it's not enough to know that the place you are right now is no longer where you want to be – this place of stuckness, foggy windows, and obstacles. you must also know where you want to be *instead*.

the future has a direction. use that picture – that dream or vision, that destination – to act like a beacon for you to move toward... let it help pull you out of your stuckness, like moths to a flame.

we RISE when we have a place to rise to.

where else might this be true?

there is a saying that goes: **how you do anything is how you do everything.**

i think this can be a helpful tool of awareness... it can offer us a helpful clue to the actual source of the muck we're in.

have a think about the stuckness you are experiencing and ask yourself: where else might this be true? how else might this be showing up in my life? where else do i feel this stuck?

after my period of grief and depression i found myself longing to get back to my business, back to my unfinished projects that had been put on hold, and back to this book in particular.

but every time i sat down at my desk i just felt stuck. i would stare at the pages, i would stare at the screen... i would feel like it was *all too hard* and then i would go back to my bed and my netflix.

and then one day i had a little AHA. i sat down at my desk to deal with some paper work for my dad's estate... i stared at the pages and felt like it was *all too hard*... the exact feeling of pain and avoidance and wanting to bury my head in the sand that i had been experiencing with my work!

i was avoiding the paper work to sort out my dad's finances and estate – an admittedly difficult, painful job – but i realised i was also avoiding all 'paper work': my book work, my year planner, my website updates... all of it.

the story i was telling myself about my dad's estate – "*i just can't handle that right now*" – was essentially me saying "*i can't handle any of it*"... not my book, not my work, not the finances... none of it.

what is true for one thing is true for all things.

how we do one thing is how we do all things.

what is happening here is happening elsewhere.

this can be true for how we behave, react, respond... what we experience, accept, reject... the way we approach or handle things... who we are being or how we are living.

i think often times we tend to partition the various aspects of our life – work, home, family, friends, self, finances, hobbies, relationships, etc – but this strategy asks you instead to **look for the thread lines that are common.**

for instance:

→ if you are unable to accept help with a task, where else are you unable to accept help?
→ if you are lazy with a small thing, what big things are you being lazy with?
→ if you are being really critical of yourself, where else are you feeling criticised?

→ if you are avoiding a particular job, what else are you avoiding?

→ if you are experiencing shame or conflict or judgement or anxiety or fear in one part of life, where else is it showing up?

when we look for these patterns we can find clues to deeper things we might be stuck with... the true source of the issue... and that helps us figure out what we need to heal or shift. perhaps we can even make little changes in lots of places in our lives to help with the stuckness we feel – come at the issue from more than one angle! and we can also create more integrity and alignment in how we live, behave, and act... in all areas of our lives.

when something isn't working, ask: *where else might this be true?*

sticky steps.

there are actions that you take every single day that keep you in the place that you are. (whether you are aware of them or not!)

i think of these as sticky steps.

sometimes we can trick ourselves into believing that *we are doing things. we're taking steps! we're so busy busy busy!* but the question for you to consider is: are your daily habits, behaviours, and actions actually moving you forward to where you want to be or are they 'steps' that actually keep you stuck.

if you imagine your stuckness as a big muddy puddle... are your steps and actions actually helping you to get out of that puddle or are you just sliding right back into the muck?

this strategy is simply about **being aware of the habits that keep you stuck**. awareness, as we know, is the first step!

for instance if you are working on building worthiness and confidence in yourself and you know that every time you go on instagram you find yourself mindlessly scrolling feeling more unworthy with every image – you compare yourself or feel like you will never measure up or start to wonder why you even bother – then the instagram habit is a sticky step.

if you are working on being less of a people pleaser or working on creating better boundaries around your time and how much you are willing to give – but every morning you start the day by having a coffee and reading through your emails and messages and find yourself overwhelmed by all of the people you have to respond to – then the morning email habit is a sticky step.

have a think about your habits: when you wake up, how you start your day, your meal times or break times, how you end your day. think of the actions that you repeat daily, weekly, monthly. think of your common behaviours and routines.

ask yourself: *are any of these things that i do by force of habit or same old routine keeping me in my stuck place?*

awareness is the key. often times just being aware of one of your sticky steps is enough to help you do that thing less often!

when i made the decision to get back to my work and to get back to this book – after such a long period of letting myself stay stuck and small and safe – it was quite hard to let go of my sticky steps, they had become such a subconscious habit: stay in bed, scroll social media, binge watch netflix, drink wine until bedtime, scroll social media, sleep poorly. repeat.

one night as i was lying in bed i could smell cigarettes, so strongly! no one in my house smokes cigarettes, but my mom did her whole life – she died of lung cancer – and it is a smell that drives me crazy. i tried to say: *hi mom, thanks for visiting, i love you and know you are with me, but please send me a different sign when you are near!* no luck. for days i kept smelling cigarettes. i felt like it was a message, like she was bugging me on purpose, so in an effort to figure out what my mom wanted me to know i started to track whenever it happened.

the cigarette smell happened when i was hiding in bed, scrolling social media, avoiding the world, sinking back into my stuckness.

long before she died, my mom was stuck. she had so many things she loved and still wanted to do: she longed to travel, to get back to gardening, to start painting, to organise more visits with loved ones, but she just couldn't seem to overcome her inertia. she was on her own journey of grieving, depression, and giving up on life. the cigarettes were part of her soul journey and they were a way to knock me back onto mine… they were mom's way of reminding me of my pledge to her to help people – and myself – get unstuck. as i finally began to work on this book again, and make plans for my next steps forward, i haven't smelled the cigarette smoke since.

once you are aware of the sticky steps that are keeping you stuck, what can you do?

it can be hard to completely **drop an unhelpful habit** – try replacing it with a better action. for instance instead of waking up and picking up your phone to check instagram, pick up a book instead, or pick up your journal and a pen.

it can also be hard to just **add in a new positive habit** – try adding it on to an action that you already take. try tapping in the shower, or try making a gratitude list with your morning coffee.

to **catch yourself in a sticky habit** – try wearing an elastic band on your wrist and snapping it whenever you find yourself taking an action that is keeping you stuck.

and remember to be kind to yourself. you are learning a new way of moving forward. an unhelpful habit may be something you've been doing for years and years so be compassionate to yourself when you notice you are taking a sticky step.

this isn't about *breaking* habits… there is no pressure here to suddenly quit something cold turkey or to suddenly start perfectly doing something new instead. it is about untangling all of the threads and exploring all of the layers of whatever has you stuck.

sticky steps are simply another way for us to stay safe in what we know.

be careful of defending your 'steps' with very good reasons to hang on to them: *yah but i need that time* to shut my brain off. i need to keep myself distracted, away from my spinning thoughts. i need something mindless, frivolous, safe, comfortable.

sticky steps can keep you distracted from inner work that you may need to do. we must face the things that show up in our lives — **we must feel it to heal it** — and if we don't, it will just come up again and again until we do.

actions that are actually distractions — avoiding or procrastinating — can indeed feel so good: safe, mindless, comfortable... but at some point you will have to take a real step forward.

so be honest with yourself and be aware of your sticky steps. each bit of awareness you gain is like loosening up the panels of the box you've been stuck in. soon you'll break free.

play bingo.

this strategy is a fun one... not only is it wonderful for awareness, but it is also really fabulous for changing that *stuck, yuck, ugh* energy into something more playful, fun, and even humorous!

here's how it works: grab a piece of paper and some pens.

have a think about whatever has you feeling *stuck, yuck, ugh* right now... something that is bringing up frustration, fear, worry, doubt, lack, overwhelm, or fear; something that you want to clear or shift or unstuck so that you can truly RISE.

consider your particular stuck situation and start making a list of everything and anything that does or might happen to keep you in that stuck place.

you can think ahead and make predictions, you can look back and think of what's happened in the past, you can think about what is pushing your buttons you right now.

it can be something that comes from inside of you, or comes at you from others, or simply shows up around you in some way.

consider...

- comments, remarks
- actions, reactions
- behaviours
- patterns, habits
- thoughts, beliefs, feelings
- situations, provocations
- frustrations, fears, worries, doubts
- home, work, community, social media feed, etc.

just jot down anything at all that comes to mind which is associated with the stuckness you feel. there are no wrong, silly, or unlikely ideas – if they pop in your head as something that does or might happen, it's worth adding it to the list!

this list is your **BINGO card.**

now you get to play the game... **the noticing game.**

pop your list – your BINGO card – somewhere you can easily refer to, perhaps in your day diary or beside your bed or in your wallet.

as you go about your daily life notice when those things *do* happen... notice the 'BINGOs.'

→ that comment that you knew was going to push your buttons? BINGO!
→ that voice of the inner critic inside your head piping up? BINGO!
→ that thing that your boss does every single time? BINGO!
→ that old habit that is so hard to break? BINGO!

you get bonus points in this game for actually saying the word out loud. trust me, there is something powerful in actually shouting out: BINGO! at least try shouting it loud in your head... BINGO!

remember: this is about noticing. it's about awareness.

when we make the list – when we predict all of that stuff that is adding to our stuckness – we are exploring and realising what keeps us in our stuck little box or what adds to the layers of fog that cloud up our windows.

as we play the game of bingo we begin to notice more and more... you might find yourself even adding to your bingo card, or calling BINGO on stuff that you hadn't initially included on your card!

bonus points for that too. nice awareness!

but some other really wonderful things happen when we play BINGO.

as i mentioned already, the energy of this stuckness begins to change. you can't yell BINGO! – even in your head – without feeling at least a little bit playful. you might even find yourself laughing at yourself a little!

you might find that you become even more curious about your BINGOs. you might find that you congratulate yourself when they happen: you predicted it, you are so awesomely aware, well done you!

putting your 'stuff' down on the BINGO card takes the power away from those buttons a little... your inner self begins to believe: "hey, i got this!"

and that is another bonus of this game. when you put your stuff down on the card, your brain immediately begins to look for solutions for that stuck stuff. the moment you write down: "she is going to say... and then i am going to feel... and then i will..." your brain is already finding a way out, your brain is already making a plan: "ok then, maybe instead i could..."

suddenly, with your BINGO, you have:

    a. more awareness
    b. a more light-hearted approach
    c. a plan to start changing the way you handle it!

the BINGO game works in so many situations. you can apply it to:

→ something you feel stuck with right now – procrastination, avoidance, resistance, blame, etc.
→ something that you are about to do that you know is going to bring up your 'stuff' – frustrations, fears, worries, doubts, etc.
→ or simply even something in your life that you want to change your energy around – maybe a

difficult relationship, a frustrating situation, or a pattern you want to change.

try it the next time you are about to do something you know is going to provoke you in some way! see what happens.

and don't forget to use the word itself... loud and strong and playful... BINGO!

we RISE when we play and have fun!

look in the mirror.

what is happening **around us** is often a big clue for what we need to work on **within us**... particularly when a situation or a person is really pushing our buttons in a big way.

if you find yourself really stuck in a situation... feeling annoyed, angry, hurt, frustrated... unable to let go, unable to move on, unable to detangle yourself... this is where you need to do a little more exploring!

look in the mirror.

those provoking people and situations are often a mirror for something we need to see within ourselves... and often what we need to see and work on is not that obvious! this takes some detective work, some deep exploration.

keep in mind that if there wasn't something you were meant to see or learn or explore you would move on from those situations more quickly... you would be able to let go, ignore, or simply focus on yourself!

often when we are feeling provoked we say phrases like: *he made me feel like... why does she always have to... when is he ever going to... why can't she just...*

in other words our focus is all on another person. it's time to turn that focus inwards – to hold up a mirror so that what we see instead is ourselves.

we can use the clues of what we've been saying about others to look in the mirror – to look inside – and see what there is to see.

for instance:

- the pain you are experiencing may be a reflection of a wound you need to heal
- the criticism or judgement that is upsetting you may be a reflection of the voice of criticism or judgement in your head
- the anger you have at others may be a reflection of where you are angry at yourself
- how you want to make someone else feel may be a reflection of how they made you feel
- how they made you feel may be a reflection of how you are feeling about yourself deep down

not all mirrors point to **something inside of you that you need to heal or clear or 'work on'**... a mirror can also point to something you need to recognize or embrace within you.

for instance:

when we feel annoyed by someone else's 'shortcomings' this can be a clue of **something we are not honouring or recognizing in ourselves...**

- it could be a strength that we have, something we are good at — we get annoyed because we don't realize that this is something that doesn't come easy to everyone
- or it could be a shadow part of our self — something we haven't wanted to recognize within ourselves, and it's time to embrace it.

the reflection can also show us **something that we need to do next...**

- what someone is not giving you may be a reflection of what you need to give yourself
- what you are wanting to receive more of in your life may be a reflection of what you need to be giving out to others

the reflection in a mirror works because light bounces off of the mirror and back to our eyes. this is such a good reminder that the light we see in others is the light that is within us, the darkness we see in others is the darkness within us.

sometimes people and situations show up in our lives to be a mirror for our inner selves... there is something we are meant to see.

the only person we have any sort of control of in this world is us. the only person we can change is us. the only person we can 'force' to see things differently is us.

where do you have a mirror in your life right now? what do you need to see... to recognize, explore, heal, clear, shift, honour, embrace.

as you begin do this mirror work you will find that feeling of being provoked eases up. if it doesn't, not a worry... it's just that there are still layers to peel away!

keep asking the question: *what do i need to see here? what else is going on?*

we RISE when we get curious.

body wisdom.

another way to gain awareness about our stuckness is to check in with what our bodies have to tell us.

we can get clues from physical sensations such as tightness, tingling, pressure, discomfort, tension or stress, pain or ache, heaviness or weight. we can also get clues from disease, ailments, and physical conditions.

a few years ago i decided that i wanted to do something about a number of spots that i had on my skin. i discovered they were little flat warts and made an appointment with my doctor to have them treated medically: some warts were treated multiple times and still wouldn't go away. other spots weren't treated at all as the doctor didn't think they were in fact warts.

i had a thought in the midst of all of this treatment to see what the emotional, mental, and energetic aspects were for this condition. according to my research, *warts are little expressions of self-hate: feeling unworthy and inadequate, focusing on the negative or ugly aspects of life.*

as i read about the meaning behind the warts i made an instant decision: i would make a change in my life... i would focus on self-love and worthiness. i didn't know *how* i would do that yet, i didn't make any plans or work out any strategies. but i *decided*. self-love and worthiness would become my mission.

a couple of weeks later i was getting my nails done and realised that the wart on my hand was gone! it was one of the persistent ones that survived multiple treatments... and it was suddenly gone!

my heart was beating fast... i wondered when it disappeared, i wondered about all of the other ones! the second i got into my car i checked for them... all of the spots were gone! even the ones that had never been medically treated. even the ones that weren't actually warts.

this is the power of our awareness. i hadn't really made any changes to my life, i hadn't even tried any strategies yet, i just became aware of the issue of self-hate and unworthiness and made a decision to make a change.

and the warts were gone.

i did indeed go on to practice self-love and self-worth (you can find those strategies later in the book)... i wanted those warts to stay gone, so i stuck with my commitment to work on worthiness.

but even with that work, one day my warts came back. there were dozens of them, all along my right arm, directly along the lines of a tattoo i have which is a memorial to loved ones i have lost. the warts appeared sometime during my period of depression after i had been home to canada for a funeral.

i hated them, and i wanted them gone, but had no idea what to do about them medically given their location on the tattoo. i researched again about the meaning of warts and the significance of the arm but couldn't see what change i needed to make... i think i was just too lost in my darkness.

then one day, about a year after they appeared, i touched my arm and realised they were gone. they had appeared quite suddenly while i was grieving the loss of a beloved family member and the loss of my dream to move home to be with my family. they disappeared just as suddenly sometime after i found out my mom had terminal cancer and i went home to be with her.

in hindsight, i believe the warts were about focusing on the ugliness of life, and since they were growing on a tattoo honouring love ones lost i think they were about focusing on the ugliness of death as well. arms are about missing out on wonderful things because of internal limitations and conflicts.

when i knew i was about to lose my mom i made a conscious decision while i was with her to take a mental photograph of every beautiful thing i witnessed in her final months with us. i began to actively look for and record the beauty in life and the beauty in death, and those moments, though incredibly bittersweet, still comfort me.

i believe that decision – to find the beauty in life and death – is what made my warts disappear. and to this day, i gently rub that tattoo on my arm and pray that i may keep noticing that beauty.

i share this story in the hopes that it will encourage you to explore the information your body holds for you! try this:

have a think about the stuckness you are feeling right now. focus on it for a moment – focus on that ugh-yuck-meh feeling that it brings. once you are holding onto it in your mind and in your heart... check in with the rest of your body. notice where your attention goes... notice any physical sensations in your body or notice any physical conditions that come to mind.

the first thing you notice is the best thing. go with that! trust what your body is wanting to show you.

you can use the books mentioned below to check in with the meaning and the message of that condition or body part, or you can check with google, or you can trust your own intuition. the more you tune into your body's wisdom the stronger the connection will get and the more you will understand the message for you.

after years of working on this, i have noticed now what a variety of sensations in my body mean for me. one that i commonly get is a feeling of pressure around my forehead like a tight hatband. for me, this is a sign that i am NOT being aware of something, i am NOT noticing something. another is goosebumps... i heard someone once call these truth tingles, i love that! goosebumps are a message of "yessssss! that's it! pay attention to that thing.... ooooh that's juicy."

you might feel something in your ears (is there something you aren't hearing?), in your throat (is there something you are not saying?) in your stomach (is there something you are not digesting or assimilating?) or somewhere else.

alternatively, if there is a physical ailment that you are working on healing right now with a doctor, medical intervention, or treatment you can check in with the emotional, mental, and energetic healing that you can focus on as well. you can support your healing with even more awareness and a commitment to do the inner work as well as the physical.

please note that i am not a medical intuitive – i.e. i am not an expert in the wisdom of the body or the way our trauma and stuckness can show up in our body – i am simply curious to learn and explore. the two books i mention below have helped me in my own journey and are a good starting point.

please also note that i absolutely encourage and support traditional medical knowledge and intervention as well. if you are experiencing a condition or ailment, any kind of disease, discomfort, or pain, please see a doctor. give yourself your absolute best chance to heal and have a long, healthy, vibrant life.

what i have shared here is simply meant to be a strategy for awareness and exploration... practice tuning into your body, practice exploring the messages that your body has for you, practice trusting your body and being an advocate for your own health and healing. and practice doing the inner work that supports whatever else you are doing for your physical self!

***

play more: two books that may be helpful for interpreting the wisdom of your body are <u>the secret language of your body</u> by inna segal and <u>you can heal your life</u> by louise hay. both books have helpful A-Z indexes to check in with the parts of the body and the various ailments to learn what information is held there.

muscle test.

muscle testing is a technique from the field of applied kinesiology. i must note that i am not a kinesiologist, nor do i have formal training in this field. but i have learned and used self-muscle testing as a strategy for awareness and exploration and i want to share it with you!

muscle testing is a way for accessing and getting answers from your subconscious mind — bypassing *conscious you* to check into the beliefs, emotions, and knowledge that is held by your subconscious self, your body's innate intelligence, or your soul.

essentially, you ask your body questions and you get clear answers! by practicing self-muscle testing you can explore what is at the core of your stuckness.

muscle testing works with the electrical system and the muscular system of the body on the premise that:

→ when you make a statement that is *true* the energy of your body flows and the muscles are strong
→ when you make a statement that is *false* the electric circuit of your body temporarily short circuits and the muscles weaken.

a simple self-muscle test that i love to use is done by creating interlocking chains with your fingers and thumbs: with your non-dominant hand, touch the ends of your pinky finger and thumb to create a circle shape. like making an 'ok' sign - only use your pinky & thumb. with your dominant hand, make a 'chain' with your fingers by touching the ends of your pointer finger and thumb to create a circle that is linked with the circle in your other hand. like making an 'ok' sign – only linked with the other fingers.

your fingers will make a 'linked chain' shape like this:

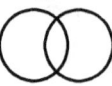

this is your basic self-muscle test position. you don't have to squeeeeeeeze your fingertips together, tight and intense. just hold them in a comfortably strong position.

test it out by making a statement you know to be absolutely true. try for instance stating your name: "my name is ____." try to pull apart your hands and notice that your fingers stay strong and your circles stay linked, or locked.

now try making a statement you know to be absolutely false: "my name is jo smith." try to pull apart your hands and notice that your fingers are weak and your circles are broken, or unlocked.

this is very easy to try but it does take practice to become accurate and consistent, and to begin to trust the answers.

you need to be able to get out of your own way. it helps to approach this strategy without any sort of attachment to the outcome or 'answer'; instead focus on a simple desire to learn, to have awareness, or to uncover a truth.

it also takes practice to get good at the questions you ask yourself!

yes/no or true/false type questions work well:

→ the strong lock/link position is a yes/true answer
→ the weak unlock/unlink position is a no/false answer

be careful not to ask 'future' based questions – i.e. "will i..." – this is not fortune telling! ask questions about **you right now** – i.e. "am i/do i..." – or about something from the past that might be affecting you now.

the idea is to focus on just one issue or situation – something you are wishing to shift or heal or get unstuck – and explore what may be going on subconsciously.

some questions you might try:

- do i have a limiting belief about ____?
- am i willing to let go of ____?
- do i feel safe to ____?
- am i ready and able to ____?
- do i need to forgive myself for ____?

you might start by practicing and testing some things you already know to be true and false and just get good at asking those types of questions and testing the responses. practice allows you to relax and let your subconscious answer instead of overthinking or trying to 'lock up' your muscles.

as you practice and get better at muscle testing, you might like to ask if your body is responding with 100% accuracy. being tired, thirsty, or worn down can affect your responses; ask your body to respond 100% accurately. you can also try asking about the strength of your response... for instance is your yes a 100% yes? perhaps it is only a 10% yes! the more you practice and play the better you will get.

if you are interested in exploring more check youtube for some different types of self-muscle testing... there are different finger tests, arm tests, and even standing/sway tests that you can try and you might find there is one that works best for you.

once you have found a self-muscle test that you like, and you feel like you are getting consistent, accurate results, this can become a helpful tool for awareness and exploring.

cycles & rhythms.

as soon as you read the word 'cycle' you might already recognize in yourself a natural cycle or an inner rhythm that affects your life. perhaps you aren't quite aware of exactly what that looks like or how it works but you can sense that you have it.

for instance:

- times when things flow, and times when they don't
- ups and downs of your energy levels, your emotions, your mindset
- stages of doing, trying, creating, birthing, taking action and stages of retreating, being, waiting, reflecting, rest
- periods of feeling optimistic, hopeful, positive and periods of having a 'baditude', feeling negative or dejected

awareness of how and when and where these periods occur for you can be so helpful... you can begin to honour your inner rhythms rather than trying to fight them, you can work *with* them for more ease and sustainability.

and you may learn that your stuckness is not necessarily a reflection of what is going on inside of you, rather it's about how you are effected by the natural rhythms and cycles of life.

try this: for the next few months keep track of your natural cycles — your ups and downs, your backs and forths. if you have a sense that your energy levels seem to have a natural cycle to it, track that. if you notice that your mindset or your moods seem to have a recurring pattern, track that!

you can keep track in a calendar or daily planner... at the end of the day simply make a note for yourself. after a few months of tracking you should begin to notice your natural rhythm, and the more awareness you gain as you go the more you can work with it.

you can also look back at your road so far to look for patterns. as i was looking back in my old notebooks for the things i wanted to add to this book i noticed a repeating pattern of periods of ignition — feeling powered by my mission, blasting full speed ahead, nothing could stop me — followed by periods of retreat and rest. i had been worried that i was stuck in inertia, but noticing that this is perhaps a normal cycle for me helped me to embrace my period of retreat and honour that i simply needed rest and space to heal.

it can be a powerful reframe to see that perhaps your stuckness is simply part of a normal cycle that you are in. it can also help you to move forward and to plan ahead... i will remember now that there is a season for ignition and a season for retreat and both are an important part of how i work!

there are some known cycles that may affect you – i will share the energy for these different cycles to offer ideas and so that you can check how your own cycles may overlap these ones. but keep in mind that you might notice something different in your tracking!

moon cycle

i heard it described like this once: the gravity of the moon affects all of the water on earth, and humans are made up mostly of water, so why wouldn't the moon affect us?! i have noticed, for instance, that i have insomnia during the full moon, which affects my energy, which affects my stuckness.

new moon = a 'blank page' for beginnings, intention setting

waxing moon = action taking, momentum

full moon = illuminate the darkness, release what doesn't serve your intention

waning moon = reflection, gratitude, surrender, rest & restore

hormonal cycle

pre-ovulation = ideas, intentions, beginnings
ovulation = fertile, create, take action
pre-menstrual = hone, refine, declutter,
menstrual = rest, rejuvenate, heal, release, clarity

seasons

spring = planting seeds, beginnings, emerging
summer = growth, implementation, fun, play
autumn = harvest what you've sown, abundance
winter = hibernation, reflection, retreat, rest

planetary cycles

you've probably heard about 'mercury retrograde', you've maybe even noticed the effects! retrograde simply means a change in the movement of the planet throughout the sky. you might notice a sense of chaos during a planetary retrograde.

search online to find out when each of the planets is in retrograde and notice the effects on...

mercury = communications
venus = relationships
mars = energy, passion, action
jupiter = expansion, freedom, wisdom
saturn = justice, karma
uranus = individuality, self-expression
neptune = inspiration, dreams, intuition
pluto = transformation

numerology

each year has its own universal energy due to numerology, which works on a 9 year cycle. to learn the numerology of the year, simply add up the numbers in the date. (2020 = 2+0+2+0 = 4 so 2020 is a 4 year.) you can also learn your personal year number based on your birthday, as well as the numerology of specific dates. search online to explore numerology further.

1 = beginnings, opportunities
2 = connection, co-operation, relationships
3 = creation, expression, socialising
4 = building foundations, simplicity
5 = change, expansion, freedom, travel
6 = responsibility, nurture, family, home
7 = reflection, introspection, re-evaluating
8 = expanding, ambition, achievement, leadership
9 = completion, closure, endings

calendar year

for instance, the school year has its own cycle of work and rest. if you are a parent with school aged children, or if the work you do is affected by the school year, it is worth exploring how this cycle affects you. or you may notice how someone else in your life has a strict 'calendar' cycle that affects your family or your life (for instance you work with a shift worker, someone who flies in/flies out, or has a certain busy/quiet periods to their work year.)

daily cycle

there is an energy to the different parts of the day... early morning, mid-morning, mid-day, afternoon, late afternoon, evening, night time, and through the night. how does your energy fit with the energy of the day?

universal cycles of change

creation = beginnings, the start of a journey

growth = development, planning

steady state = sweet spot, moving forward as planned, complacency

turbulence = system too complex, become lax, problems develop

chaos = things fall apart, tail-spin, time to take control

dropping off = acceptance, letting go, moving forward, make a change

meditation & dormancy = inward silence, just BE

as you become more and more aware of your own natural cycles you might also become aware of other common cycles that overlap with yours... take notice! anything that helps you work with your own rhythm is helpful to creating more flow and less stuckness!

***

play more: i first learned about how we can work within our hormone cycles from rebecca campbell's book <u>rise sister rise</u>. i heard about the universal cycles of change on natalie sisson's podcast: nataliesisson.com/when-too-much-change-is-dangerous/

part two:
shifting strategies

rise.

creating change.

awareness is just the first step of the self-leadership journey. now what do you do with what whatever you have become aware of?

your next step is to take the initiative to **shift, heal, clear, release, transform, finish, or change** things... in some way.

you know that you are stuck. you know that you aren't shining your light the way you long to. and now – with a toolbelt full of awareness strategies – you can explore that stuckness, peel away the layers, see what there is to see.

but just knowing something is there doesn't take the emotional weight away. so now what?

you've uncovered memories, stories, thoughts, beliefs, patterns, attachments... fears, worries, doubts, frustrations... what do you do?

we RISE when we shift what stands in our way.

in this section of the book i want to share some more tools with you, more strategies you can learn and practice for shifting that stuff... you can apply each of these to nearly anything you notice and want to heal, clear, or change.

let's first think about the word 'shift'.

i use it here to simply mean 'work on your stuff'. what that means to you, what that looks like for you, well that depends on you! as you will see later in this book, i think we need to choose, and define, our words wisely.

i also use a variety of words here interchangeably — just in case one resonates with you more than others! note that all of these words are verbs — action words — i think this is important too, because it reminds us that we can actually take action, we can DO something... the inner work is actually work that you *do*!

to shift means to change. change gears; change position, direction, tendency, frequency; to exchange or replace.

to clear means to remove obstructions or unwanted items; to get past something safely; to become free of something; to gradually disappear.

to heal means to become sound, healthy; to alleviate pain, anguish, stress; to mend, restore, improve; to make better.

the sense of the inner work we are here to do, i love the definition of healing as the process of becoming whole or of coming back to your true self.

rumi[3] says: "*the wound is the place where the light enters you.*"

so healing is simply allowing the light to enter: to illuminate the darkness, to bring all the parts of you together to become whole again, or to allow your true self to shine through.

healing is NOT about fixing you. you are not broken.

this is about releasing or embracing or transforming or dissolving the blocks or the 'fog' or the 'box' that is keeping you stuck or preventing your light from shining bright.

remember: your light is there. the path forward is there. we simply need to clear or shift whatever is in your way!

the strategies listed here offer ideas for clearing things physically, emotionally, energetically, even spiritually.... because we need to cover all of our bases and we need to throw everything at our stuff that we can. some may work better for YOU... so be open to learn and explore as many tools as you can!

some of these strategies may be familiar to you, some of them may be brand new. i encourage you to either amp up your existing efforts in some way — add new layers of intention to your practice — or to try something new! you never know what will work best for you if you don't try it.

these strategies can easily be combined with each other as well as with the strategies for awareness in part one and some of the specific unstucking strategies we will learn in part three. in this way, you can create your own unique, powerful practice for RISING.

***

play more: do you have your own strategies, tools, and tips for shifting and healing? do share them with us using the hashtag #iamariser... we can always add new ideas to our toolbox!

be intentional.

no matter which strategy you try, your success will come with your intentions.

if you don't believe it will work – if you are just going through the motions, or if you don't actually want to shift your stuff – the strategy is not actually going to help much.

so be intentional with your efforts!

set a clear, strong intention for what you want to heal, clear, release, finish, change, or shift in some way and be truly willing and open to the strategy helping you do that.

to be more intentional with your efforts here are some ideas to try:

ritual

a ritual is simply a set of actions performed regularly, repeated for a specific purpose. a ritual doesn't have to be religious or 'woo woo'; for instance, when you light a candle and turn on soothing music and pour a favourite drink to go with your hot bath... you've just created a ritual. you have made your bath more intentional, you have given it meaning beyond the simple act of getting clean!

the thing to remember with rituals is that it doesn't actually matter *what* you do, as long as it is **meaningful to you!**

if you want to try these healing strategies down by the sea with the waves at your feet washing away the fog... you've just created a ritual. if you want to add candles or music or meditation or crystals or essential oils or anything else that has meaning to you, please do. if you want to do these strategies on certain days of the week or month, or even at a certain time of the day... go for it!

rituals can include location, sacred space, speaking, writing, physical objects, physical movement, date or time, or anything else that adds meaning, adds intention, or sets the stage for your efforts.

prayer

i will preface this idea by sharing that i am not religious, i don't attend church, i don't follow any traditional or organized belief system.

but i absolutely believe that we are connected to something bigger than us, something both outside of us and within us. call it god, universe, source, spirit, divine... to me it's all *light*, just as our soul is light. you do you... do 'connection' however it suits you; define ideas of spiritual practice and prayer however it suits you.

here is an idea that i love: prayer is when you talk to god, meditation is when god talks to you... prayer is talking, meditation is listening. this is why i am including prayer as an idea for being intentional with your strategies, because i think that **saying out loud what you are ready to shift** is so powerful.

call it an invocation, a declaration, an affirmation — you don't have to call it a prayer — but a simple intentional statement can have great meaning and add power to your efforts.

for instance you might try:

→ with arms wide open, i am ready to...
→ please change me into someone who...
→ please help me to...
→ ... and so it is, and it is so.

what else would support your intentions to shift, clear, heal, release, stop, or change whatever is keeping you stuck? there may be something you are already into that you can add to your efforts, with even more intention. or you might want to explore something new.

essential oils can be a powerful, intentional tool to support your efforts. they are one of my personal favourites... in fact i am using oils even as i am writing this book: i am using ginger which is the oil of empowerment, because my wish for this book is to empower people... to put actual tools into their hands that they can use themselves and that will make a difference in their lives.

music is another powerful intentional tool that i love to use, spotify is a great place to create playlists that match your intentions.

when i sit down to write i have my own short ritual that includes meditation, an invocation, essential oils, music and coffee! these things set a stage, they give meaning to my work and to my space, and i feel ready.

what else can you add to your efforts? if you do self-reiki, work with meridians, practice yoga, love elemental space clearing, are interested in feng shui... add *that* to whatever strategies you try!

***

play more: my favourite book for exploring the emotional intentions of essential oils is <u>emotions & essential oils: a modern resource for healing</u> published by enlighten alternative healing. there are oils to support pretty well anything at all you might be working on within yourself!

choose an anchor.

one powerful strategy to be more intentional with your efforts to get unstuck and to RISE is to choose an anchor.

an anchor is a physical talisman or touchstone that represents or reminds you of your intention... something you can truly hold on to or say out loud or see right in front of you.

and an anchor can be anything you want it to be — anything that is meaningful and powerful to *you*.

first, try to get really clear on your intention:

→ what is it you want to remember?
→ what are you working towards?
→ what do you want to focus on moving forward?
→ what is your goal, your desire, your vision for yourself?

once you are clear on your intention, choose your anchor... or perhaps let your anchor choose you! often the first thing that pops into your mind when you consider what would be a great anchor for your intention is the best thing for you.

here are some ideas for what you might use as an anchor...

words

i love to choose a single word as my anchor. for instance, i always choose a word for the year... i love having that one word to guide my path and anchor me back into my goals and dreams for the year. alternatively you could choose a phrase, a mantra, or even make up a hashtag for yourself. the more you say it out loud, write it down, display it on your walls... the more powerful the anchor is!

objects

crystals are a great physical object to use as an anchor as each crystal has its own meaning... its own properties. i personally love to use jewellery as an anchor – each time i touch my ring, my necklace, my bracelet i am reminded of the meaning of that piece... i come back to the intention i hold for myself. colours can be powerful anchors too – each having their own meanings and associations – so you might choose an object for its colour.

scents

scents are very powerful anchors, tied closely to our emotions, to our memories, to our desires. a friend of mine asked the other day: *"what does your goal smell like? mine smells like the beach!"* and i LOVE that! i have already mentioned the use of essential oils and you will see them mentioned throughout this book. but you can use scented candles, scented soaps or lotions or sprays, or you can choose specific flowers and herbs for your space.

songs

music is another powerful anchor – again closely tied to emotions, memories, and more. choose a theme song for yourself (for your goal or your intention) and play it every time you need to get back to that ignited feeling, back to your light. if you need some music inspiration, check out the #lighthouserevolution spotify playlist at karengunton.com/free

images

vision boards are a very popular tool for anchoring into your goals and dreams... we know they work! but you can simply even choose one image or photo to represent your intention: a photo that reminds you of what you are working towards, a photo of a person who inspires you, or a photo that symbolizes your why.

animals

animals can be powerful totems – each evoking their own meanings, symbolism, and intentions. you might already have an animal totem that appears in your life – find out what message that animal has for you. or you can choose one as a talisman – wear your animal in some way or display it in your workspace.

symbols

symbols, sigils, or marks can be a powerful way to activate your intentions. try designing your own sigil or choose a design, pattern, or symbol that has particular meaning to you. draw it to activate it; wear it, display it, or store it somewhere safe if you like; or try burning it or releasing it in some way to let the universe fulfil your intention.

i created my own symbol for the phrase: *i am a riser* which you may have noticed throughout this book. i love it so much i will probably get it as a tattoo! i also make morse code bracelets that use a pattern of dots and lines to create a 'secret' message that has meaning to me but still looks really nice to wear.

anchors are completely personal so choose whatever you like. **it has meaning because you say it does.** the point is to choose something that will remind you of the work you are here to do, the change you want to make in yourself or life.

use your anchor to remember where you want to go, who you want to be, what you want to do or have, and why.

give yourself something solid and powerful to hang on to as you find yourself tossed by the waves, hammered by the storm, or lost in the darkness. something to remind you of your light: your strengths and gifts, your purpose and passion, your goals and dreams.

your anchor will bring you home again... back to your light.

even though i wrote the book on being a lighthouse – standing tall and lighting up – i don't always get it right. like everyone, i have crap days. i feel tossed by the storms of life. i get off track and forget to shine. i respond to challenges and annoyances from a dark place.

i love what gabby bernstein[4] says: *"it's not about living in the light all of the time, it's about your come back rate."*

our challenge is to catch ourselves in that downward spiral, or that dark place, or the middle of that storm, and to choose to come back to our light.

hang on to your anchor, let it bring you back.

we RISE when we have something to hang on to.

forgiveness.

there is one healing strategy that i truly believe helps with absolutely anything that may be going on for us.

forgiveness.

many times when we hear that word — forgive — we can get a little defensive: *why should i forgive that person or that situation? they don't deserve it!*

this is the most important thing to realize about forgiveness...we don't forgive for the other person's benefit, we do it for ourselves. **WE deserve it.**

with forgiveness, we are not saying: *it's ok that you did that, it's ok that that happened.* we are simply **accepting that it did indeed happen** and we are ready to move forward now.

forgiveness is a way to let go of the weight we carry around with us — a sort of emotional or mental decluttering. it's a way to change the energy around something that is blocking us. and a way to clear the fog that prevents our light from shining through.

another thing can happen when we hear the word forgiveness. we might think: how do i forgive a fear? how do i forgive an old story, an old pattern, a limiting belief? isn't forgiveness for PEOPLE?

here is my take on it: **when i do forgiveness i do it *for* me, and i do it *to* me.**

if it is a fear, a limiting belief, or a layer of resistance... i picture forgiving my inner self, my soul, the 'real me' that lives inside. i ask her to forgive outer, imperfect, human me for letting that thing block my path or for hanging on to it for so long or maybe for not being aware of it.

my favourite forgiveness practice is called ho'oponopono. it goes very simply like this:

i love you. i am sorry. please forgive me. thank you.

when i do this practice i simply say the words to my inner self until i feel the energy of whatever it is i am stuck with begin to change.

i believe that this particular combination of phrases is powerful...

- *i love you:* start with the energy of love. try to find one thread of something you love or at least appreciate about the person or situation.
- *i'm sorry/please forgive me:* you take responsibility for you. the only person you can control or change is you!
- *thank you:* finish with the energy of gratitude. appreciation helps to shift resentment.

but you can change this up if you like! choose your own words of forgiveness or create your own forgiveness mantra, prayer, practice, or ritual!

try...

→ visualise your inner child or future self and say the words to her

→ visualise a beam of light and love being sent out to heal/clear whatever you are forgiving

→ write down everything associated with what-ever you are forgiving then recite the mantra - burning or erasing or tearing up whatever you have written

→ use the mantra while tapping/EFT or while doing reiki or some other practice you love

→ use the mantra while running, or walking, or moving your body in some way to help shift things

→ use the mantra while in the shower or the ocean... picture the flowing water washing away the pain of the issue and leaving nothing but learning/awareness/understanding behind

→ sing the mantra (you will find a song version of ho'oponopono at karengunton.com/free)

- → visualise the mantra healing whatever part of your body you are holding this resistance/stress/trauma in

- → use essential oils to support you in your forgiveness – thyme is the oil of releasing and forgiving

- → write a letter to a person associated with whatever you need to forgive... let it all out! and then forgive. and remember the forgiveness is for you, not them... burn the letter instead of sending it if you wish.

- → use the mantra to make a list: everything you love about yourself, what you are sorry for and what you need to forgive yourself for now, and then everything you are grateful for. self-love and gratitude are powerful practices on their own, why not combine them with forgiveness for an even more powerful practice

my point is that the practice itself will have more power if it feels powerful to you... the words will have the intention that you give them! so make this your own, make it something that is truly a 'how' – a tool in your toolbelt. there are lots of great books and talks on forgiveness, it is a practice that is growing in popularity, so do explore and play with how to make it work best for you.

i was recently listening to a podcast about apology and found that it was really pushing my buttons. i felt so uncomfortable, i just wanted to turn it off and pretend that there was no one i needed to apologise to! one particular situation was playing in my mind as i listened... it was one i had been trying to forgive for a long, long time.

as i listened to this podcast i kept thinking: *i am NOT in the wrong here! i do NOT have anything to apologise for!* of course my strong reaction was a clue that i did in fact have some work to do; i forced myself to listen and be open to learning and then got really honest with myself about what i contributed to that difficult situation. it turned out to be a very powerful exercise, the missing link in my efforts for forgiveness... i needed to understand not only what i was forgiving them for but what i was sorry for myself.

perhaps forgiveness is a practice you have already been using. can you take it to a new level in some way? create a personal practice or ritual that feels even more powerful to you.

perhaps these four simple phrases seem *too* simple to be powerful. i get that, i thought that at first too. but honestly, i have seen situations change before my eyes when using this mantra, in ways that can't really be explained except that the energy of the situation truly shifts when we practice forgiveness.

***

play more: i first learned about ho'oponopono from joe vitale's youtube video <u>healing with ho'oponopono</u>.

listen to brené brown and harriet lerner's two part workshop "i'm sorry: how to apologise and why it matters" on brené's podcast: <u>unlocking us</u>. brenébrown.com/unlockingus

cord cutting.

people come into our lives for a reason. we experience the situations we experience for a reason. they offer us an opportunity to learn. they offer us a mirror... a way to look at ourselves and see what it is we are meant to heal, explore, or shift.

but what do you do when you've done the learning, you've explored your stuff, you've reframed the situation... and you still can't seem to move on?

if you find yourself endlessly thinking about, remembering, obsessing over, being provoked by, or blaming someone else... or something else... then it's time to cut the cords.

if you can't seem to break an old pattern, change an old story, or start fresh with a new way of doing things... then it's time to cut the cords.

cord cutting is like decluttering your energetic space. no matter what kind of relationship we have with people or with situations we form energetic bonds with them − and the more energy being sent between, the stronger those bonds form.

so even if you have learned from it and you are ready to move on − maybe you've done some mindset work to reframe the situation into something more positive; maybe you have made some practical decisions to create some distance or change your reactions — that energetic cord can make it feel like it's still pulling you back in.

this is where it is useful to have some sort of cord cutting exercise or visualization in your toolkit... try out some different ideas to find one that feels right to you, or create your own! a google search on 'cord cutting' will give you all sorts of ideas.

i actually do a visualization that is more of an **untangling** than a cutting.

i like to picture myself standing tall like a lighthouse, beaming my light outwards. and i picture the other person/situation also as a lighthouse, off in the distance, doing the same... and all of our beams of light are entangled and twisted like strings of rope. i visualize pulling my beams of light back into my own lighthouse: as i breathe in i kind of suck my beams of light back into me, and as i breathe out i blow their beams of light back to them.

i like this visualization because it acknowledges that everyone has a right to be their own person, their own lighthouse, and you can't actually change *them*... you can only change *you*. change your energy to untangle from theirs.

it also acknowledges that the stuff that's come up — the situations/words/behaviours/actions etc. that have pushed your buttons in some way — have all happened for a reason. you were meant to learn, to grow, to evolve... and now that you have you can send that stuff back to whoever brought you the lesson.

i do this 'cord untangling' as part of my daily meditation practice, but it is a great visualization to do before you fall asleep or to do in any moment of your day if you feel sensitive to someone else's energy or provoked by someone or something. take the learning, leave the energy behind.

what other strategies can you play with for breaking energetic ties? try:

→ use essential oils: oregano is the essential oil of non-attachment

→ call upon the archangel michael to help you cut the cords with his powerful sword

→ grab a white board and draw out/mind map the energetic ties you are ready to change — brain dump everything associated with that situation, let it all out. then use the eraser to sever the cords

→ add an invocation: i bring my energy back to me, i take responsibility for my light. i send your energy back to you, i am not responsible for how you choose to shine.

i will share my full cord untangling exercise with you… may it help you to release whatever ties that bind.

note: the following guided visualization is available as a recording that you can listen to – grab it now at karengunton.com/rise or try reading through and visualizing as you go.

close your eyes. picture yourself as a lighthouse. feet solid on the ground, spine straight like a tall tower rising up from the earth, a beautiful blue sky above, waves gently lapping at your harbour.

picture the light with in you, burning softly but so bright. this is the light of your soul. imagine that light beaming outwards from your lighthouse tower… from your belly, your heart, your throat, and your forehead.

now picture other lighthouses dotting the harbour. these lighthouses represent the people or situations in your life. you might choose to identify one now, specifically. what is the situation that you are choosing to untangle from now? picture the energy of that situation… that particular lighthouse is standing tall across the harbour, beaming light outwards, and it's all tangled up and twisted in with your light beams, just like cords of rope.

take a deep breath in. as you do, visualize pulling all of your beams inwards back to your lighthouse…

your breath is sucking all of your light back to you, back home.

take a deep breath outwards. as you do, visualize sending their light beams back to them... your breath is like the wind blowing their light back to them.

keep breathing in and out with that visualization. as you do, as you send a breath their way, wish them well.

you could try saying something like: "nothing but love for you, i send you back to your own path, good luck with all that you do, you are free to go and shine your way." or "thank you for the lessons you brought my way, thank you for showing me what i needed to see. i am ready to move on now from this energy."

keep breathing and untangling your beams of light until you feel the weight of that energy leave you. once you feel like your cords have separated, feel that other lighthouse fade out of your awareness... the harbour becomes dark again.

take another deep breath in and visualize that breath fanning the flames of your inner light, the light of your soul. with a deep breath out, visualize your light expanding and expanding and expanding... filling up your whole lighthouse with light.

visualise a beam of light going down through your centre and connecting you deep into the earth. feel the earth rising up to support your lighthouse.

visualize a beam of light connecting you to the sky above, to your source. picture beams of light coming down from the sky through the top of your head, filling up your lighthouse with even more light.

with each breath in allow your light to burn and burn as bright as possible, and with your breath out you can begin to beam your light outwards again. as you do – as you start to beam your light outwards – picture those light beams acting just like a garden hose... when your light is flowing outwards no other light can be flowing inwards back to you.

breathe in and expand your light, breathe out and beam your light outwards, brighter and stronger.

as you expand your light, as you take up space with your energy, as you beam your light outwards to touch others in the way you were born to do... visualize those beams as hoses where no other energy can be flowing back into you... these powerful hose-like beams help you to protect yourself from being entangled with their energy again.

you can visualize this the next time you come into the view of that particular lighthouse again in the future... remember that you have already untangled the cords and your light is now a hose that can only push outwards.

remember you are the keeper of your light.

you have the power to protect and direct your light and your energy.

you are untangled. you are free.

surrender.

for me, surrender means that i recognize that i don't have to figure it all out, in fact i can't... i can't possibly control everything. surrender means i get to stop efforting... i get to take my hands of the wheel.

surrender means letting go of...

- attachments to outcomes
- the need to know
- the need to be right
- the need to have things a certain way
- the need to have things happen in a certain time frame
- the need to do it all and figure it all out by yourself
- old bullshit stories keeping you same, stuck, small, silent, scared

often times it seems like surrender happens as a last resort.

we hit rock bottom, we find ourselves in the lowest of the low, and as we break down we surrender because we recognize there is nothing else we can do. we are done.

but we don't have to wait for rock bottom! we can practice surrender at any time. in fact the more we practice it, the better we get at it. and the more we find a way to do 'surrender' in a way that resonates.

i must admit this is one strategy i find hard to practice... it seems very intangible to me, but i think that is partly due to my personality. i like being in charge, so taking my hands off the wheel feels tricky.

in order to surrender you need to be **willing to let go**. it helps to recognize that your tight attachment to all of that stuff is actually not serving you and that there is a better way. be willing to explore the possibility of that better way.

in order to surrender you need to **feel safe** – safe with the unknown, safe with allowing, safe with NOT having everything figured out and tightly controlled. it usually feels safer to hang on to the old, it's what we know!

the pain of staying where you are has to outweigh the pain of change. and the lightness, the freedom of letting go has to feel better than the need to hang on... it helps to **have hope**! a hope that things will feel better when you let go.

it also helps to **have trust**. as much as taking your hands off the wheel is about giving up control, control is not the opposite of surrender. trust is! so how can you build trust... in yourself, in others, and in everything around you?

i think it helps to **have something to believe in**... to have faith and trust in... something to surrender to:

- something inside of you... your higher self, your wise self, your soul, your instinct, your intuition;
- something outside of you... your guides, the angels;
- or something bigger than you... god, source, the universe, the earth.

whatever your belief, an idea to try is to *let go and let god*. my mom used to say this phrase and i love it, it reminds me of the whole point of surrender. or you can use a different mantra: *let go and let soul. let go and let love. let go and let spirit. let go and let light.*

try creating your own surrender ritual, something that feels powerful, intentional, and concrete:

→ make a list of every attachment, every 'need' you are ready to surrender – and do something to symbolically let go... burn the list, or cross out each item

→ let the shower wash the attachments away; stand in the waves and visualize each wave washing them away; go for a run and visualize letting go each time your foot hits the pavement

→ visualise handing over each item from your list to whatever higher power you believe in (apparently archangel zacharael is one to call on for surrender!)

- → make a pile of rocks for each burden, frustration, worry, fear, doubt you carry. throw them into the sea, a lake, a gully, or an empty field one by one to let each one go.

- → try an invocation: arms wide open i give this over to you, i take my hands off the wheel, i surrender my burdens, worries, fears, attachments. i open up my heart and surrender to you. i let go and let god.

- → try a "change me prayer": divine light, change me into someone who surrenders my attachments. change me into someone who can let go.

- → try a mantra: i surrender. i surrender. i surrender. i surrender. i surrender. say it until you feel your energy change... that sort of rock bottom feeling of letting go

- → use essential oils to support your intentions: wintergreen is the oil of surrender, it can help you let go and trust in a higher power

- → use music to help you surrender, choose a song that feels like letting go and letting god.

as you practice strategies for surrender, notice how it feels for you. do you notice a difference in your body? do you have a release of emotions? do you feel lighter or perhaps more at peace?

anchor into what you notice, it will help you to affirm the power of surrender and it will strengthen your practice for next time!

we RISE when we let go.

***

play more: i first learned about change me prayers from the book <u>change me prayers: the hidden power of spiritual surrender</u> by tosha silver.

tapping.

tapping, or emotional freedom technique (EFT), can be a very powerful tool to add to our toolbox of strategies. i love recommending it because it is something that anyone can learn and try, and it can be used for literally ANYTHING you want to shift in your life. it is a simple tool that can put the power to clear, heal, transform, or get unstuck into your own hands.

please note, i am not a tapping expert. i have studied the practice with a variety of teachers and i am a fan of the technique myself so i like to share it as a possible tool that you can use to help yourself.

EFT uses a combination of positive psychology and the meridian/energy system in the body (think along the lines of acupressure points) to relieve, release, transform, or heal whatever we are suffering with. it is a way to reset both the body and the mind from whatever we are blocked with.

use it to:

- build confidence, worthiness, belief, mojo
- shift old stories, limiting beliefs, blocks, fears, doubts
- heal underlying emotional issues, trauma
- create change
- move forward

it works by **tapping into our negative emotions** – fear, anxiety, limiting beliefs, memories, unresolved issues, etc. – by speaking them out loud, and by **tapping into our body's energy system** by tapping on the meridian endpoints.

these nine endpoints are found on your hand, head, face, collar bone, and under arm.

to practice tapping you must first identify the thing you want to focus on – the problem, issue, or stuckness – the thing you want to clear or shift or heal or change.

i find that it helps to have a list ready of all of the aspects that layer into this issue so that you can tap on them specifically, as well as a list of positive things you want to affirm or believe so that you can move forward.

(this is where your awareness strategies will help!)

when you tap you start with statement like this:

even though i (specific thing i am stuck with) i deeply and completely love, honour, and accept myself.

the first part of this statement **acknowledges the stuckness you feel** – you honour the place you are in, you bring your feelings to the surface.

the second part of the statement **provides unconditional love, compassion, and acceptance for yourself** - which is healing in and of itself!

you then tap gently but firmly on the meridian points as you speak out loud first all of the negative aspects you are looking to shift, followed by the positive aspects you wish to remember moving forward.

often times, as you are tapping and speaking out loud, new things will start bubbling up to the surface... you become more aware of all of the layers underlying your stuckness as well as the things you can focus on as you heal.

tapping is something that you can do anywhere, anytime, for anything. if you are out in public and need to tap on something, for instance to reduce your anxiety or to relieve your stress, you can just tap on the karate point on your hand if you'd like, as it is more unobtrusive.

when you first try tapping it can really help to have a script to follow. i have created a simple 'tapping to get unstuck' resource that you can follow along with at karengunton.com/free – it will help to learn the meridian points and the specifics of the process.

as you practice tapping you will get better at creating your own scripts and drilling down to the core issues underlying your stuckness. note that having perfect phrases/word choice is not the important thing here — what matters most is your ability to tune into the emotions underlying your issue, to understand the deep meanings/feelings behind the words you are using.

you might find that you need to tap on the same issue again and again in order to move yourself up the scale out of your stuckness and move yourself forward. as you tap make note of the new things that come up so that you can tap on them some more the next time around.

i have found that it helps to make tapping a daily practice — try doing it when you first wake up or right before you go to bed or in the shower, or add it into an existing practice, perhaps after your meditation.

you can also combine other practices with tapping... you can do EFT while also doing forgiveness, cord cutting, surrendering, or any other healing strategy listed here.

once you give tapping a try you will begin to feel more comfortable creating your own scripts and focusing more closely on your specific emotions and situations.

***

play more: go to karengunton.com/free for the free video & worksheet that accompanies this chapter on tapping. it will help you to learn the tapping points and the process for tapping to shift your stuckness.

my absolute favourite tapping teacher is brad yates on youtube. he has a script & tapping video for just about anything you can think of and he has a beautiful and kind vibe. his videos are generally around 5-7 minutes in length – totally doable – and a great place to start.

emotional release.

we know from our awareness work that there is all sorts of stuff that can keep us in a stuck place... stuff that we carry around with us, and perhaps have been carrying for a long time... stuff from the situations, stories, patterns, people, even from ourselves, that layer on top of each other. we can carry a weight of anger, frustration, blame, hurt, shame, guilt, comparison, judgement, unworthiness, and more... it is heavy and burdensome and it does not serve us to keep holding on to it all.

it helps to have a strategy for letting go by letting it out... once and for all.

a strategy for emotional release.

often when we think about allowing ourselves a big emotional release – perhaps by confronting someone and telling them what we really think – it isn't actually about releasing things for ourselves it is about trying to change them, or make them feel bad, or make them sorry.

the strategy i want you to consider now is not about that. it is about truly letting it all out... *for you*. letting it go... *for you*. so that you can move forward without the weight of the stuff you've been carrying. it is meant to be healing to you, cleansing for you, and empowering for you.

it's about *you*. not *them*.

the only person you can change is you.

so this strategy is about allowing yourself a big emotional release, without the drama of actual confrontation, while keeping yourself safe, and with the intention that you do this for you. not for them.

consider what you have been holding on to, what you have been pushing down inside, what you have been swallowing, what you have been carrying around with you for months and years, what you have been avoiding or brushing under the rug.

that is the stuff we want to clear out.

try:

→ **write a long 'fuck you letter'**

write to the person/thing you are angry with... even if that person is yourself! actually write this letter out. there is more power in handwriting than there is from typing. let yourself do some free-writing, without censoring, without editing. just write and let it all out. then try burning or releasing it in some way to let go of the energetic ties to that person or thing.

→ **go for a long drive by yourself**

imagine the person is sitting next you in the seat. let yourself say everything that you have been swallowing down. shout, swear, be angry, be sad, be annoyed, be honest! don't just think it out but actually speak it out, say it out loud. there is power in using your voice, more power than we often realize.

→ **say it all out loud in the shower.**

there is a cleansing quality that occurs in the shower that goes beyond your body and a bar of soap! letting your words out and letting them echo into the shower and letting them wash away down the drain... that can be so cathartic!

→ **scream into your pillow**

perhaps even use your pillow as a punching bag if you need to. there is something very healing that comes with a physical release (not just a verbal one!) afterward, take your pillow out into the sun and fresh air to release all of that absorbed energy.

→ **visualise**

create a scenario with your imagination for release. for instance, try imagining yourself as a big fat firehose that is swollen with unreleased water... it's time to turn on the tap and let it all flow out until there isn't a single drop left. add in a physical action (such as writing or running) that represents that symbolic flow you visualise.

→ **write the book**

there is something powerfully healing and cathartic about writing and sharing your story. you don't even have to let anyone read it. though if there is one other person you feel safe giving your story to, that can be healing too... to get it out and to be witnessed. but honestly just the act of writing the story – figuring out all of the pieces and how everything unfolded and the stuff that was said and the stuff you didn't say and what impact it had on you and how your life changed and what you know now – all of it comes together to give you awareness and the act of writing it all is a massive release... the book is done and you are done with it too.

→ **creative expression**

write and sing a song, perform a dance, create a work of art, explore with photography or design, build something, take something apart, sculpt, knit, draw, paint... whatever calls to you. creativity can be a powerful way to express your emotions and let your feelings flow.

→ **cry**

maybe this one is obvious, but so often we avoid it. i actually do cry often and i cry easily – i tell people i just happen to feel everything through my eyes – but at the same time i avoid stuff that i know will reaaaaalllly make me cry, because it is exhausting! but crying is a really good way to release. if you need some help, choose a movie or something that you know is going to activate those feelings, memories, and tears... perhaps a conversation with that one empathic friend you've maybe even been avoiding because you know that as soon as you start talking you will start crying.

→ **use essential oils**

support your intentions to release: cilantro is an oil of release and can help with feeling liberated, unattached, lightened, and cleansed; thyme is the oil of releasing and forgiving and can help you find and empty the soul of all negativity and trapped emotions.

an emotional release can be incredibly draining — especially if you let those tears flow or let the punches flow or let your voice flow. no matter how you decide to try this strategy you will likely feel drained.

but think about that visual of the fire hose… feeling drained is the point! we are releasing until every backed up, blocked off drop has been released. if you feel totally drained, exhausted, spent… congratulations. you did good.

follow up this strategy with some massive self-care and self-compassion. lots of water, rest, time, space, comfort, grounding… whatever you need to fill your bucket again. but this time we are filling it with the good stuff. the stuff that will serve us moving forward, instead of the crap we've been carrying around for so long.

time to let that stuff go.

check your bucket.

speaking of buckets... how's yours?

you need to be a **conscious caretaker** of your bucket — recognising when it is empty, knowing what fills it up, being choosy about what you allow to take up space.

i like the visualisation of the bucket — it helps me to think about what i am carrying around with me, what i need in order to fill up again, and also what i have got to give. you might prefer a different analogy: some people talk about cups (you can't pour from an empty cup), spoons (how you spend your limited spoonfuls of energy), or batteries (what charges you vs what drains you). you might even like to think of your whole body as a bucket or as the vessel that carries your load.

what does your bucket (or version of a bucket) look like?

how big is it? what is it made of? how do you carry it? does your bucket feel light and easy or heavy and cumbersome? does it feel secure, protected, strong or does it feel fragile, leaky, precarious? how does it feel when it is full of good stuff? full of crappy stuff? completely drained empty?

close your eyes and have a think about this for a moment — visualise your bucket and how it feels in your mind's eye. perhaps grab a notebook and pen and write about it or sketch it out.

as a conscious caretaker, you get to decide how that is working out for you as well as any upgrades that you need to make. you are welcome to trade in your bucket for another one! maybe one with a lid so that you get to decide what goes in and what gets drained out.

build your own version of the bucket that you need in your life.

and then consider this about yourself...

→ what fills up your bucket – in a good way? how does it feel when you have a full bucket?
→ what drains your bucket – in a not good way? how does that feel?
→ what are some (perhaps neutral) things that sometimes fill your bucket too full – in a not helpful way?
→ what is it like for you when your bucket feels too full of way too much and you just feel overwhelmed or you feel depleted?

keep in mind that you can carry a physical load, an emotional load, a mental load, and/or an energetic load... so do explore what might be in your bucket.

how you answer these questions is quite specific to you. if anyone has ever told you that you ought to do a certain act of self-care and it just kind of makes you shudder to think about (for me it is massages or baths) then you know that what fills one's bucket is not the same for everyone!

that is why it is important to know about your own personal **bucket fillers, bucket drainers, and bucket overwhelmers.**

as an example – time with good, close friends may be a bucket filler for you. but time with groups of people you don't know well, introductions and small talk, may be a bucket drainer... you might be able to do it just fine, but recognise that it does drain you and you need to recharge after that. and if you are feeling really depleted or overwhelmed in some way, then time with close friends might actually feel like too much... like you just can't manage anything else in your bucket right now.

another thing to consider are **your buttons**. what sets you off? what pushes your buttons consistently? what pushes your buttons particularly when you are depleted or overwhelmed? and when you do get pushed... whatever is inside your bucket is what comes spilling out! what is it like when you are at your worst?

alternatively, what are **your sparks**? these are the little things that light you up or remind you of who you are. they can help bring you to a state of calm, safety, confidence, courage. think: *i feel most like me when*.... what is it like when you are at your best?

when you know your own bucket you can become a better caretaker of it. this can be particularly important if you are experiencing depletion, exhaustion, burnout, stress, overwhelm, over giving, difficulty receiving, or shutting down. but you don't have to wait for your bucket to be dangerously full or empty, you can practice being a good caretaker right now!

i think it also helps us to have more compassionate for others – recognising how you might be able to help fill someone else's bucket or recognising how certain interactions with people likely has nothing to do with you, it's about them taking care of their bucket.

we all carry a bucket load of stuff.

this strategy is about being more intentional with our own bucket – being choosy, being protective, and being conscientious – about what goes in and what comes out, what fills us up and what drains us, what we carry around and what we give away.

we RISE when we honour our self.

word work.

we've talked about choosing an anchor to help you as you do the work to get unstuck and to RISE. perhaps you have chosen a word to act as an anchor... what does that word actually *mean* to you? for you?

this strategy is all about being intentional with the words you use: defining words, reclaiming words, discarding words, choosing new words, maybe even inventing your own words if you like.

there are so many words used, perhaps overused, in the personal development space – many of them included in this book! – words that point to this inner work we are doing to get unstuck, to clear our fog, to shine our light.

heal. clear. shift. transform. uplevel. elevate. empower. embrace. embody. connect. expand. release. forgive. honour. own. emerge. ignite. surrender. allow. anchor.

decide: what do these things mean to YOU? and what is it that you want for you? you can't stand in your truth and focus on your intention when the words don't resonate. that's how we get overwhelmed by the 'should dos' and the comparison and the uncertainty and everything else that can get us back into feeling stuck.

success. balance. freedom. space. simplicity. flow. community. service. abundance. belonging. purpose. worthiness. safety. courage. permission. belief. certainty. creativity. play. shine.

you might also try defining your roles - you decide what to call yourself, and you decide what the definition is, or you make up your own words so that you have something that truly fits you.

coach. teacher. leader. artist. speaker. author. mentor. guide. trailblazer. revolutionary. visionary. alchemist. strategist. healer. seeker. rebel. warrior. free spirit. sage. mother. daughter. sibling. partner. friend. volunteer. boss. colleague.

i call myself an unstucktor because i help people get unstuck. words like coach and mentor don't resonate with me, so i made up my own.

what key words do you need to define for yourself? open a dictionary or thesaurus if it helps. focus on the feeling of the words for you. choose new words. make up your own words and definitions if you need to.

sometimes we need to take back the words that have been tarnished for us in some way.

i remember back when i was a school teacher there always seemed to be someone who scoffed at the teaching profession or who made a comment about my lack of accomplishment in becoming a teacher. i realised later on that i had some shame in my life around that word: *teacher*. i had to take back my ownership of that word, i had to stand in my own truth of what that word means to me, and i had to heal that old bullshit story of shame and lack associated with the word.

sometimes choosing a new word, inventing a word, or writing a new definition can be just the thing we need to change the energy of our stuckness. i listened to an interview with two brothers who described how they chose to call the depression/anxiety/sadness they often feel "the woog." in using this word they could simply say: *it was the woog. the woog is here for a visit. we need to talk about the woog.*

perhaps consider giving your own personal brand of stuckness its own unique word or name... see if it changes things up for you!

the thing about doing word work is that we don't ever need to let any word define us. we get to choose. we can say no to the words and definitions that are keeping us boxed in or stuck or foggy. we can own the words that not just define who we are now but exemplify who we want to be. we can chose words that help us to make sense of our place in the world or give us a sense of belonging. we can give ourselves words that lift us up and help us to stand tall, in strength and alignment... words that help us RISE don't let words be another box that keeps you small and stuck. you get to choose. do some work on your words – when you come to peace with them they are not so volatile/scary/constricting. your words have power. choose wisely!

we RISE when we find words that set us free.

sign a new contract.

you've been living with and conforming to an agreement — a contract — one that you wrote yourself, perhaps without even realizing it.

it's a contract that states who you are allowed to be, where you are allowed to go, and what you are allowed to experience, achieve, explore in this lifetime.

is this contract something that you want to keep honouring? do you want to keep living under its rule? do you think it is serving you well?

if not, it's time to tear that contract up and write a new one.

start by first thinking of your current contract — the one that constrains you, the one that no longer serves you. what does it say?

what are the beliefs, thoughts, emotions, stories, behaviours, responses, actions, reactions that have been ruling your life?

what so called 'rules' have you been living by — rules like the "shoulds" and the "musts" that come up over and over again in life?

try playing in the space of contrasts to work out what exactly was in the old contract and to get very clear on what needs to go into the new one.

i call this **the contrast game.**

for example...

→ what am i being? who do i want to be?
→ how does this feel? how do i want to feel instead?
→ what have i been talking about? what do i want to talk about instead?
→ how do i spend my time? how do i want to spend my time instead?
→ what am i doing right now? what do i want to be doing instead?
→ what thoughts keep playing in my head? what thoughts do i want instead?
→ what have i been believing? what do i want to believe instead?
→ what story have i been telling myself? what story do i want to write next?
→ what have i been valuing? what do i want to value instead?
→ what do i focus on? what do i want to focus on instead?
→ what do i have around me right now? what do i want to have?

keep going with these questions and make up some of your own!

anything that you notice about your stuckness right now – the agreement you've been keeping with yourself – ask: *what do i want instead?*

the new contract should not just be about what you want... this isn't a vision board. this is a new agreement that you are making with yourself, with your soul, with your inner wise self, with the universe.

your new contract should be about what you will take responsibility for, what you will actually do, what you will say, what you will believe, what you will know, what you will be.

you might even spell it out, as though it is your new 'user's manual' for your life, moving forward...

- when this happens _____ i will...
- when i notice that _____ i will...
- when i am feeling _____ i will...

actually writing this stuff out, like a contract, is not just a physical action you can take right now to take responsibility for making changes, it actually maps out those changes! you can use the new contract, a physical document written by you, like a handbook for your next steps.

you might want to write a letter to yourself or to the universe to make a strong statement about your new contract.

dear universe, i have made a mistake! i gave you the impression that i _____. i am ready to create a new agreement with you. this is what i actually want: _____ and these are the steps i will take: _____

what are you putting in your new contract? how does it feel to have some new rules to live by... a new agreement to honour?

pick a new job.

it's your choice.

you can see the stuff that comes up in your path as either an **obstacle that blocks you** or a **sign post that guides you** and points to your next steps.

think about the stuckness that you have been exploring... the layers of awareness you have been peeling away. think about your perspective of that stuff. how does it all feel?

it is such a bummer to be stuck, i get that. that's why i am writing a whole book about getting unstuck, and why i call myself an unstucktor. this work matters.

but it is really hard to do the work when it all feels very yucky and hard and UGH all of the time. try to stop swimming in the UGH of the stuckness and instead focus on the gift of it!

it is coming up now for a reason... **it *is* your next step.**

my favourite way to do this – to see my stuff as a sign post on my path instead of the obstacle – is to **give it a new job.**

whatever 'fog' you are exploring right now... whatever stuff you are shining a light on... give it a job so it stops getting in your way and is helpful to you instead.

for instance, when i feel resistance about something (those feelings of worry, fear, and doubt) i choose to see that resistance as a sign that whatever i am doing *matters*, it is what i am meant to do! if it didn't matter i wouldn't feel any resistance.

when i feel jealous, that is a sign of something that my soul is longing for, something that i want for me.

when i feel shame, it is a reminder that i need to focus on compassion and do some serious self-love work.

when my inner critic gets loud in my head, that is a definite reminder that i am not listening to inner wise me, lighthouse me. the volume of her voice has been turned right down! oooooops!

when i feel particularly annoyed by a person or a situation, it is a sign to tighten up my boundaries.

when my buttons are getting pushed, that is a sign of some inner work that i need to do, something i need to see in me.

later on in the book i will expand on these examples further so that you can keep practicing this strategy... but the idea is that by giving your stuck stuff a new job it completely changes the energy of that stuff!

by giving your stuck stuff a new job you are taking what is happening *around you* or happening *to you* and instead focusing on what needs to happen *inside of you.*

it is a **reframe.** a way of tapping into a new perspective or a new energy.

you see the stuck stuff not as something that is *stopping* you but instead it is...

- a sign
- a reminder
- a clue
- an opportunity
- a 'shove'

... pointing you to your next steps, pointing you in the right direction, for where you want to be or for what you need to do.

so try to **flip the situation** around from the negative to the positive... look for the positive spin, or for the helpful clue, or the way forward. there are probably places in your life that you already do this – when something doesn't go your way you might say: oh it wasn't meant to be. or everything happens for a reason.

these are common reframes. you can practice creating more of them for all sorts of areas of your life!

have a think about the common 'blocks' that you've been facing, the persistent 'fog' that you are trying to clear... what new job can you give it?

the truth is this stuff will come up again and again, no matter what inner work you do. so you might as well give it a job that is helpful to you instead of it always getting in your way!

put your stuck stuff to work for you!

it can help if you have some positive reframes ready in advance. that way, when that stuff comes up again, and it will, you can be ready... armed with a new perspective and a new job.

make good choices.

choice has been a big theme in this book! for most of the strategies shared here i think we could include the phrase: *choose wisely*. or as i like to say to my kids every time they leave the house, very loudly and obnoxiously with a big smile on my face: "MAKE GOOD CHOICES!"

our stuckness, and our capacity to RISE, boils down to self-responsibility... you are the only one responsible for your thoughts, feelings, mindset, actions... only you can change you.

so let's explore three ways that you can indeed make good choices.

choose the upward spiral.

you might have heard of this idea before referred to as 'above the line' vs 'below the line' thinking/feeling. you could also think of it as choosing to 'go high' vs 'go low'. i like to think of it as choosing the upward spiral instead of the downward spiral... this reminds me that one little step upwards or downward leads to more of that direction.

what this choice requires is for us to understand that every thought or feeling has a counterpart that can be a more helpful, or upward, choice. when we choose the upward spiral (the more helpful thoughts or feelings) we can actually pull ourselves up out of the downward spiral (or less helpful thoughts and feelings.)

for instance, if you find yourself stuck in a cycle of resentment it probably started with one thing... one instance of frustration, bitterness, discontent. once you begin to spiral in resentment, it builds... you find more and more things to be resentful about, you sink into what i call *the baditude.*

for me, it starts with something stupid and small, like socks left on the floor. and then it grows when the dishes don't get put in the dishwasher, and then i find myself stomping around the house, slamming cupboard doors resentful of every single job i do, every way i have to take care of everything, and the way no one else cares, clearly! i sink into the resentment downward spiral quickly, and it snowballs fast.

a way to shift into the upward spiral, to move out of the space of resentment, is with appreciation. it might start with finding just one thing to appreciate about the person or situation you resent, but once you begin to choose the upward spiral it builds... it expands... and you can find more things to appreciate.

when the little things tip me into a resentment spiral i am trying to catch myself with a simple phrase: *i appreciate this home.* i appreciate this space we have, this space we share. i appreciate my family is here together, safe and healthy and happy. it reminds me that socks and dishes aren't all that important in the grand scheme of things. i do still yell at everyone to do their god damn chores and pick up their bloody things, but at least i am not in a spiral of resentment... my baditude shifts more quickly.

try thinking of some of the downward spirals that you often find yourself in and ask: *what is the counterpart? what would help me choose the upward spiral?* here are some ideas to get you started, though you might find that you need to create your own counterparts.

resentment – appreciation
control – trust
vulnerable – safe
despair – hopeful
judgement – acceptance
scarcity – abundance
blame – responsibility
anger - forgiveness
fear – love

know the fine line.

similar to the concept of the upward vs downward spiral, there are some feelings that are quite similar, but when we look closely one is a more helpful (upward) choice than the other... and often it is a fine line between the two.

guilt and shame are two feelings that are sometimes described interchangeably, however do have a fine difference. guilt means: *i did something bad.* shame means: *i am something bad.* guilt is helpful, it shows us what we did that we need repair, restore, or rectify. guilt helps us to grow, move forward. shame is not helpful, it eats away at our worthiness, at our sense of self, and our capacity to heal. shame keeps us small and stuck.

another example with a fine line is **disappointment vs self-pity.** disappointment is specific: *poor me, something went wrong.* self-pity is global: *poor me, everything is wrong. nothing good ever happens. no one can understand.* we can move through disappointment – we can learn from it, grow, do better. self-pity is terminal – we seek sympathy, yet cannot accept it because no one else could possibly understand.

one more example is **nervousness vs excitement.** at first glance it may not seem like there is a fine line here, but the body responds to both feelings the same way: heart races, butterflies in tummy, clammy hands, jittery, heightened state, lay awake at night visualising the future. nervousness keeps us small and safe and stuck. excitement allows us to move forward, to RISE.

anytime you find yourself stuck, ask: *is there a fine line here? and can i choose a better word for how i feel?*

let intention be your guide.

being intentional is one of our helpful tools for shifting out of stuckness. when you are intentional – when you set a clear intention for how you want to feel, or who you want to be, or where you want to go – you can let that intention guide your choices.

→ if your intention is to be brave, ask: *am i making the brave choice right now?*
→ if your intention is to be creative, ask: *does this choice allow for creativity?*
→ if your intention is to heal, ask: *is this choice healing to me?*

use your intention – your word – to make good choices. when you are feeling indecisive, return to your intention: *why are you doing what you are doing? which choice aligns with your intention?*

as i have been working on finishing this book – after taking a long break from my work – i have been feeling so indecisive about every decision and quite disconnected from my purpose, from my why. i heard a musician say in an interview: *i wanted to be on the radio, i make no apologies about that choice.* this was a total AHA for me... reminding me of what i wanted.

i wrote this book for me.

after the wreck, this was the book i needed to heal, to get unstuck, and to RISE. as much as i hope this book helps someone else get unstuck, right now in this moment, i am doing this for me... i am doing this to remember that i am a god damn RISER.

having a clear intention makes making good choices so much easier!

we RISE when we choose well.

rewrite the story.

we know that the first step in healing is awareness and we now have tools to help us achieve that awareness. but sometimes, even with awareness...

→ we can doubt what happened *(maybe i am blowing it out of proportion?)*
→ we can push aside the depth of our feelings, bury them under the rug *(it's in the past, i should be over it by now)*
→ we can absorb whatever happened to our core *(it's my own fault, it's because i am broken, wrong, not good enough etc.)*
→ we can try healing strategies yet find that we still can't change the energy of what happened

if any of these things feel familiar, consider the one story from the past that seems to be at the core of your current stuckness... you just can't seem to move on.

this strategy involves travelling back in time, right back into that story, with the advantage of taking with you your new, more self-aware headset, knowledge, and hindsight.

it is something that may help you...

- shift from what is *wrong* with you to simply what *happened* to you
- shift from feeling like a victim or passenger to feeling more empowered.

try using a journal or a sketch book or a voice recorder as you do this strategy... any tool that will help you to go through these three steps of healing your story.

step 1: observation

time travel back to the story that you would like to focus on. it might be one major moment or it may be a number of smaller incidents that add up to paint a whole picture. (the bonus of time travel is you can just pop right back to any of those moments, in quick succession, as needed!)

as an observer, a time traveller, watch the story unfold. recall the events with a new level of awareness and clarity... a keen eye for anything that was happening at the time and the way the little things added up.

do not just witness behaviours, actions, words... allow yourself to witness the full range of emotions involved. honour each emotion as it arises and remember that feelings are for feeling! we need to feel them to heal them.

observe – from a wiser, more self-aware point of view – how perhaps everything that happened wasn't necessarily *all about you*... observe with compassion how other people's pain or hurt or stuckness may have contributed. and remember that whatever happened is not a reflection of who you really are, it simply just happened.

as an observer, record the events that occurred, the depth of feelings, and the factors involved. for bonus points **tell this story** to someone you trust. for even more bonus points tell the story again and again and again

saying it out loud helps you to hear your own story. the more times you tell the story the more the pain/hurt/fear/sadness begins to loosen its hold over you. you become even more of an observer — a simple story teller — rather than a broken, hurt, scared person.

you might even notice that you begin to become sick of your own story, bored of the same old bullshit. this is great! you will feel so ready to shift this out of your way once and for all!

step 2: brain swap

travel back in time, into your story once again. this time use your supernatural powers to not just time travel but also to swap your wise, self-aware brain into the body of your younger, hurt self. let your hurt self observe this time. you — wise you, future you — are going to enter the story in their place.

in fact you are going to **change the story.**

knowing everything that plays out, honouring the depth of the emotions felt, and understanding the future consequences of this event...

what will you – wise you - say and do instead? in what way can you speak up or act out from a place of strength and knowing?

once you have done and said what is needed, you get to walk away, unscathed. you get to take with you the learning, keep the bits that help you become even more amazing, and then leave the rest behind. now that you have rewritten the story, you don't have to carry the old story home with you.

try this now: write out this new version of the story, from start to finish, with the wise headset of what needs to be said and done. this is a chance to speak up, to act, from a more empowered place.

step 3: hero to the rescue!

once you have rewritten the story, with your older, wiser self running the show, there is one more job to do as a time traveller.

pick one moment in the story, a moment when your younger self needed a super hero to save them more than ever, and travel right back to that moment.

pull up along the curb, ring the doorbell, interrupt the conversation, crash the party... whatever works, just make it a grand, hero moment.

tell your younger self: *hi! it's a long story, i don't have time to explain, just know that i am future you and i am here to tell you that you do not have to deal with this bullshit anymore! hop in the car, let's get out of here!*

and then **write a new chapter to the story.**

one that allows you to mentor, encourage, honour, support, or re-parent younger you. with your new knowledge, your new self-leadership skills, how can you help them heal? how can you help them move forward with this new chapter? what needs to be said?

YOU are the hero that younger you was waiting for!

i have found this strategy to be particularly helpful when i need to feel more empowered.

i had a particular story, an experience, that i was really struggling to move past. no matter how much forgiveness, cord cutting, tapping, or letting go i tried it was a situation that lingered: my buttons were still getting pushed years later, i was clearly still angry and hurt, and it was still keeping me up at night.

this exact three step strategy is the result of me seeking out a new way to heal that old story, that situation that i hadn't been able to move on from. in three different places i got these nudges that it was time to write a new story, so i sat down with my notebook and had a play. what would things be like if i could go back to that old me in that old painful place and look at things from a new perspective? if i could respond differently, stand up for myself in a new way, walk away feeling empowered? if i could mentor that old me and save her from years of dwelling in that old story?

it worked. rewriting my story is probably the most powerful thing i have done for myself to shift that old situation. the things that used to push my buttons or knock me right back to that place don't any more. the odd time it comes up as a worry or fear i am able to quickly change course by reminding myself that is not my story any more.

i think sometimes before we can move on we need to stand up for ourselves in some way. for instance, when we...

- long to get revenge, or even things out in some way
- dwell on all the things that we wish we had said and done
- feel shame for our fight, flight, or freeze response
- have a hard time forgiving, reframing, or letting go

rewriting the story allows us to do this... **to feel empowered and then truly walk away.**

sometimes we may need to go over the new story a few times, to allow it to truly shift the old one out of the way, and to become our new truth. sometimes the new story works so well that we don't even really remember the original story anymore – we've truly erased it and built something different in its place.

but do remember, if that same old bullshit story comes up again you can remind yourself of this:

i travelled through time and changed that story. that is not my story any more.

get physical.

much of the work we have to do — the inner work to get unstuck — is emotional work and mindset work. but we can support that inner work by taking action in the physical world as well.

so let's get physical, physical! here are some ideas...

declutter.

the physical stuff in our world can weight us down emotionally, mentally, and energetically as well. doing a big declutter can be a fantastic way to support your inner work. not only do you get rid of the stuff that weighs you down but you also clear and open your space for the new!

it helps if you be intentional as you declutter and choose what you focus your decluttering on.

for instance...

if you need new energy in your work or biz: go through your office, your computer, your website, your social media and declutter the stuff that does not serve your career direction and goals.

→ if you want to create more self-love, self-care, and self-confidence: go through your closets and drawers and declutter anything that doesn't feel like an act of self-love to own and wear.

→ if you want to improve your home life: try decluttering each room and get your partner and children to help too; work together to let go of the old and make space for the new.

→ if you want new relationships or relationships that feel like a better fit: declutter your social media lists, the groups you hang out in, your phone contacts, even your calendar.

→ if you are focusing on your finances: sort through your paper work, remove old 'payee' contacts from your online banking, cancel any ongoing payments/bills that you have perhaps ignored.

change your space.

similar to decluttering, shifting things around in your physical space can support the inner work you are doing. changing up your space can help you feel a change within... it can give you a sense of a clean slate or a fresh start or a new energy. reposition furniture; move the location of the items in your kitchen, your closets, or pantry; move items around to different rooms.

you might like to explore feng shui as a strategy to support your intentions and inner work. feng shui teaches that there are different areas of a space (a home, or even a single room) for different things: abundance, fame, relationships, creativity, travel, people, career, knowledge, health, family. by learning and practicing some simple feng shui strategies you can change the energy, flow, and abundance in your life.

new locations.

sometimes a change of scenery can do wonders when we are feeling particularly stuck, blocked, weighed down, or foggy.

if you are feeling stuck with a project try taking your work to a new location; for instance, get out of your office and work in a café. if you are doing inner work on something you are wanting to clear, shift, or heal — for instance if you are doing journaling & writing — try choosing a meaningful location for that work, perhaps a quiet spot in nature.

sanctuary.

another way to support yourself and your inner work in the physical sense is to create a space of sanctuary — something that is meaningful, inspiring, healing, safe, supportive, soothing... whatever you need.

this can be a room in your home: e.g. making your bedroom or office your sanctuary. it can be a spot in one room: e.g. turning one corner of the room into your sanctuary or making an alter for the corner of your desk. it can even be something that you create when you need it: e.g. turning your bathroom into a sanctuary with candles, oils, and a bubble bath.

creating sanctuary doesn't have to be a big, expensive job. it is simply about bringing objects and items that you love – that inspire you or comfort you or make you feel loved or safe or more like YOU – into your space. if you can have one spot in your world where you enter and you feel the way you long to feel, then you've got sanctuary.

```
old anchors.
```

just as we talked about choosing an anchor to support you with your inner work, we can also have old anchors linked to our old stuff, the stuff we want to clear out now. you know how true this is if you've ever come across an old photo or object that brings up memories that you'd rather leave in the past!

physically clearing out the objects and items (even digital ones!) that are linked to whatever we want to clear out emotionally, mentally, and energetically – for instance with cord cutting or forgiveness – can be very healing.

have a think about whatever stuckness you are working on: are there any objects that act as anchors for that old stuff – any time you see it, touch it, smell it, hear it you are brought back into that old unhelpful space?

move your body.

as we are doing this inner work of awareness, exploring, and healing we can get stuck in our heads... we can even begin to feel that all we do is think about whatever it is we are working on, it becomes a little bit all consuming. moving your body is a great way to get out of your head for a while and we can actually support our inner work by taking physical action as well.

yoga is a perfect example of a physical activity that also has energetic, emotional, mental, and spiritual aspects. as you move your body you move your energy; as you strengthen your body you strengthen your connection to spirit.

but you can do this with any physical activity you love: walking, running, dancing, swimming, etc. we've mentioned that a physical activity like boxing can help you release whatever you have been holding onto. jumping on a trampoline can be a great way to feel unstuck, to create more flow, and also raise your vibration and feel more joyful.

look up

as i was taking baby steps out of my darkness and grief, back into the land of the living, i began to walk in the morning. instead of my sticky step of staying in bed i started walking my kids to school. then i started walking a little further along the path in our neighbourhood. slowly, slowly my baby steps down that path helped me to feel a little lighter, a little less stuck, a little more like me.

after months and months of walking on this path, one day i looked up and there was a kangaroo standing at the fence! i stopped to take a photo before he jumped away, and as i stood there marvelling at my little visitor i noticed the view was actually quite spectacular! a gorgeous valley turning green with the spring. the ocean off in the distance. the sun rising over the hills behind me. i had walked that pathway eleventy million times, how had i never noticed how pretty it was?

i was walking small... simply putting one step in front of the other, surviving each day. when i am in a stuck place i am only looking inwards, i am in a fog. but what i have learned is that **things start looking up when WE start looking up**... when we straighten up and stand tall, when we lift our shoulders and chin and spine. our energy changes, and our viewpoint changes, when we change our pose, our stance.

i really love this catch phrase from the tv show <u>the marvelous mrs. maisel</u>[5]; it's a reminder each time she walks out on stage: **tit's up.**

have a think about your own posture: what does feeling stuck and small feel like in your body? when you are feeling anxious, depressed, or overwhelmed where are your eyes? in contrast, what does RISING feel like in your body? can you make a conscious effort to do more of that?

we RISE when we stand tall and look up.

now you try...

these are just a few ideas to help you get physical to get unstuck — to take action in your outer world to support the inner work you are doing. but you can actually come up with your own ideas by asking yourself questions like...

- → if i am working on changing something inside of me... what can i change in my space?
- → if there is something i need to release emotionally, energetically, or mentally... what can i physically release?
- → if i want more flow in my life... how can i create more flow in my physical space?
- → if there is something i need to heal inside of me... what can i heal/fix/mend in my outer world?
- → if i want to move or shift or clear or cleanse or strengthen or support something within myself... what can i actually, physically move or shift or clear or cleanse or strengthen or support?

simply consider: *what am i trying to do on the inside? what can i do on the outside?* and then be intentional with that effort!

***

play more: to learn more about creating sanctuary, my friend helen joy butler has amazing resources at helenjoybutler.com

to create a home yoga practice to support your intentions, try yoga with adrienne on youtube... her 30 day challenges are amazing

part three:
unstucking strategies

rise. 214

specific reframes.

you now have a number of strategies in your toolbox which you can apply to any sort of stuckness... doable steps you can take to shift things so that you can RISE.

next we are going to explore some particular muddy puddles... some of the common ones that we all find ourselves stuck in from time to time. these strategies include some specific reframes as well as other practical actions that you can take: mentally, emotionally, energetically, or physically.

pick and choose the strategies that are meaningful to you! you might want to combine a couple of these together to fit your specific situation. you might want to choose one and add it on to work that you are already doing.

and you can definitely mix and match these specific strategies with the more general ones listed previously! layer the strategies in this book to create your own unique process for doing the work.

some of these ideas might be familiar to you – perhaps i call it something different, perhaps it is something you heard about, even tried, and forgot about – now is a great opportunity to once again be more intentional with your effort... to amp it up in some way.

definitely make these strategies your own. tweak them or adjust them to suit you. add new ideas as you come across them. get creative! anything that helps these strategies to be more actionable, memorable, helpful, and fun to you is what will make them more effective!

you may notice that i give these strategies a name that is catchy or memorable or even a bit silly. there is a reason for this! i know that you won't remember all of these but i hope that you will pick up on one thing that resonates right now and go off and try it... and i think you will because we notice and connect to the stuff we need right now, the stuff that solves our current problems.

but my hope is also that the other ideas remain, like little seeds that have been planted, in the back of your mind. my hope is that one day when you find yourself struggling with some sort of stuckness that you will remember the strategies that are shared here and come back to them!

we RISE when we are ready to make a change.

***

play more: do you have your own strategies, tools, and tips for getting unstuck? do share them with us using the hashtag #iamariser... we can always add new ideas to our toolbox!

jealousy.

you know the feeling... you see something or hear about something and you are hit by a wave of pure, green envy.

it is uncomfortable. your heart beats quickly. your mouth goes dry. your skin feels itchy. you oscillate between feelings of dejection *(maybe i should just give up)*, despair *(this is never going to be me)*, and defeat *(everyone else is doing a better job already)*.

it's not a fun feeling, but jealousy, envy, and comparison are actually very helpful things to experience.

because they are a sign.

the light you see in others is a sign.

- a sign of what you want for yourself.
- a sign of what is whispering inside your heart.
- a sign of the direction you can go next.
- a sign of something you need to work on.
- a sign that there is a need for what you want to do.

if you allow it, you can actually learn so much from your jealousy.

catch yourself in the moment and say thanks to the universe for putting some very valuable information in your path! then study it: what exactly has made you envious?

was it...

the person? their authenticity, vulnerability, integrity, sensitivity, courage... something about the way they are confident, empowering, engaging?

the message? the clarity, creativity, humour, inspiration... or maybe it was bold, catchy, clever, concise, shocking, or ranty? what makes it resonate?

the object? the thing they are doing, offering, creating, promoting, celebrating, working on? maybe it's their job or their process or their focus?

the activity? what they are doing right now? how they are spending their time? what they are learning or teaching or trying or amplifying?

the engagement? the support they have? the people they work with? the affirmations of 'yes please i want that!"? the partners they have found?

or maybe it's something else?

think about it... we see eleventy billion images, articles, posts, comments, offers, promotions, stories, etc in a day. most of them just skip by our view without getting to us in anyway.

if something does push your buttons, well that's worth exploring!

ask yourself: *what am i meant to learn from this? what is this trying to show me?*

jealousy can really show you some very valuable information if you let it!

watch for these thoughts...

→ i wish i came up with that
→ i wish they asked me
→ i wish i was doing something like that
→ i wish i had time for that
→ i wish that happened to me
→ i wish i could learn that
→ i wish i said that
→ i wish they said that about me
→ i wish that was my idea
→ i wish that was me

that's how we hear jealousy in our head: "*i wish that was me*". and if we let it, that can quickly lead to "*poor me*" (dejection, despair, defeat).

or we can stop that downward spiral in its tracks and remember...

the light you see in others is a sign... it is a sign of the light that is in you.

so when you think that thought – "*i wish that was me*" – be sure to notice the signs around you and listen to your inner soul whispering: *hey... i think it's time. that's what you want, now let's go for it.*

hiding.

many of us have discomfort, if not fear, about being seen, being heard... boldly shining our light. sometimes we feel discomfort about sharing one thing, but not others. sometimes we feel discomfort sharing with certain people, not others.

and the thought of pushing past that discomfort can activate all sorts of fear, worry, doubt, and lack. anything from "who am i to share this?" to "but what if people don't like me?" to "i am not good enough, ready enough, special enough."

the secret is to...

know your zones.

you may already be aware that you have a comfort zone, but what you might not realize is that your zones of visibility and voice and connection overlap your comfort zone. it is all related. that's why the thought of suddenly reaching out and connecting with someone new or sharing something important to you can really bring up your fear... especially if you attempt to push far out of our comfort zone quickly.

picture your zones like a target.

the inner most zone is

→ *where* you feel most comfortable
→ *who* you feel most comfortable with

→ *what* you feel most comfortable sharing
→ *how* you feel most comfortable sharing
→ *when* you feel most comfortable sharing
→ *why* you share what you share

and it is important to recognise all of these... your comfort comes with where, who, what, how, when, *and* why.

in other words, you might feel comfortable sharing something with a particular person but not others. you might have a way that you like to share (e.g. writing) and the thought of doing something else (e.g. speaking) provokes your fear. you might feel comfortable sharing when it is on your own timeline, but not when you are asked out of the blue.

another important thing to remember is that those zones change for different things... the different aspects of *you* that you share.

and even that can create discomfort. when you share all of you with certain people but feel like you have to hide certain parts of you with others, or feel like you have to be something you aren't... that can begin to feel pretty awful; you feel inauthentic and you feel drained.

the secret to sharing your authentic self, to connecting with others, to being visible or raising your voice is to know your zones and then **expand them gently.**

think of one thing that you would like to share in some way – maybe a story you want to tell or some part of you that you have hidden away or a secret dream that lives inside of you. now consider how that thing fits into your picture of the target – what you share, with who, and how. consider what feels really comfortable: that goes in the centre of your target; and what feels extremely uncomfortable: that goes in the outer ring.

if you try right now to jump straight into the outer ring of sharing you will definitely provoke all sorts of fear, worry, doubt, and lack. you will probably resist doing it: you will procrastinate, you will avoid, you will make excuses.

instead, push your comfort zone gently and slowly... start where you feel most comfortable and expand from there.

as an example: let's say you have the idea to write a book, but you never ever get around to starting and you definitely don't talk about this dream of yours. try to start by sharing the thoughts and ideas for your book with your best friend or partner. as you feel more comfortable perhaps you start writing and sharing with a few others via messaging or email. as you feel more comfortable perhaps you start sharing what you have written more widely on social media or a blog. as you feel more comfortable, as you've been talking about and writing about your idea, you will begin to feel more ready to write the book.

the best thing about comfort zones, and you know this from all sorts of examples in your life, is that the thing that was once very uncomfortable/scary/hard eventually becomes easy – as long as we practice!

it's a bit like going to the gym: you don't jump into heavy weightlifting and body building on your first day; you don't jump into the most challenging fitness class. you start where you are at, you start where you are comfy, and as you build your muscles as well as your experience, you expand.

visibility, voice, connection... they all work the same way.

you are here to share your light, it is not meant to be hidden inside. you are here to be YOU... authentically, uniquely, wonderfully you. but it can also be hard... and that's because of your comfort zone.

so expand gently, and slowly. sneak up gently and slowly on the fear and discomfort so that it doesn't do your head in and provoke you like crazy, making you want to stay safe and same instead.

know your zones.

we RISE when we stop hiding.

doubt.

the voice of doubt sounds like negative self-talk whispering inside your head.

it may be the *inner critic* judging, shaming, demeaning you... telling you how much you suck. it may be the *imposter* doubting your accomplishments and talents...saying you are a fraud. it may be the voice of depression or anxiety that sees the world through a *warped lens*... telling you that everything is terrible.

there are some important truths to know:

that voice is not yours, this is not the real you. yes it sounds like you in your head but it is NOT you. (remember? you met *real you* when you met *lighthouse you!*) you can tell that this voice is not you because it is mean! all it wants you to do is beat yourself up. your true inner voice – the voice of your soul – is kind. it speaks from a place of love, loving yourself up, even when it is tough love.

that voice wants to keep you safe or small or stuck. it comes from a primitive place inside of you, a strong instinct to keep you tucked away in a dark cave. you can tell because it always pipes up when you are about to or have recently taken any step forward. this voice is ultimately not helpful to you RISING.

that voice is lying. you can tell because the voice speaks in extremes... all or nothing, always or never: *you will never be good enough, you always fail, no one cares.* (notice, that mean voice is awfully confident for someone who has literally done nothing except be mean to you!) real, wise you is able to verbalise shades of grey: *ok, so that sucked. but we can fix this, we can bounce back.*

to help you move forward even when that unhelpful, unkind voice pipes up you must...

train your inner dragon.

the first step is to see this unhelpful voice as its **own persona.**

you might like to think of it as a part of you: perhaps a somewhat immature, snarky teenage version you! or you might rather think of it as something completely separate from you: like an untrained, naughty little pet... a gremlin perhaps, or a dragon.

you can probably imagine what a pet baby dragon would be like: not necessarily naughty on purpose but constantly burning everything with its fire, smoking up the cave with darkness, as it tries to protect you and keep you safe.

next – **give the voice a name** to go along with the persona. come up with something silly or fun to say out loud... because having fun helps us to change the yuck, stuck energy of our inner doubt, inner criticism, and inner judgement. you can even give that voice a new voice so that it doesn't sound like you. test it out loud: say something that voice would say in a silly high voice or a funny low voice, or do your best samuel l. jackson impression and include some 'motherfuckers'.

the benefit of recognizing this voice inside of you as something other than the *real* you is that it helps you remember that the inner mean voice has no idea what it is talking about! plus it helps you to treat that voice with some compassion, to create boundaries, and to be aware of any healing that needs to be done.

know that your inner dragon simply wants to keep you safe, small, secure, and same. so as you step towards the stuff you long to be doing, to the places you are meant to be going... as you push the upper limit of what is possible for you towards more visibility, authenticity, purpose, and growth... that inner dragon is going to rear its head, burn its fire, pull back on its leash... anything to keep you safe and small.

but remember: *you* are in charge here.

like with any little pet, you have to show them who's boss. you need to assess the situation with a discerning eye: is there any truth in what your dragon is whispering to you? is the fear real? is the doubt helpful in any way — showing you where you could build worthiness, belief, compassion, capacity, skill, or evidence?

it can also be helpful to recognize **where this voice is coming from.**

is there a past situation, memory, experience, or person contributing to these ideas that your dragon keeps whispering to you? this is an opportunity for healing, shifting, or clearing... it's time to let go of those old stories that are keeping you small or stuck... it's time for new patterns, new responses.

once you have named your inner dragon and you have assessed the situation the best thing to do is to **pick a new job for your dragon.**

remember — they don't get to drive the bus. they are not in charge. *you* are!

so what job can the dragon take care of for you (besides trying to drive)? could you assign them to...

→ go analyse the danger elsewhere! tell them to go check the danger levels on something you are doing that you feel super confident and secure about... that way dragon thinks they are helping you but *you already know you've got this.* this is basically 'busy work', just to keep dragon out of your hair!

→ show you where you should be going or what you should be doing next. remember: dragon is not going to pipe up with all of this doubt if what you are doing doesn't really matter much to you! it's only when you expand, stretch, grow, or leap that they get really worried. so when they pipe up you can take it as a sign... confirmation that *yep, this matters! yep this is definitely what i need to explore! thanks dragon!*

→ show you where you haven't been listening to the right voice. here's the clue: the louder your inner critic gets, the less you've been listening to your inner mentor – the wise voice of *real* you, lighthouse you, is getting drowned out. this is a perfect time to say *"ooooops!" thanks dragon! you reminded me of who i need to listen to. you go sit at the back of the bus while i have a chat with lighthouse me.*

and then remember to let the voice of *real you* get louder. tune into what they would tell you to do... let *them* drive the bus. inner dragon has a different job now.

i recently decided to revisit this strategy. through the months of my grief and depression i felt that the unhelpful voice in my head had changed, the lies it was telling me had changed, and i wanted to get better at recognising that voice for what it was... not real me but the voice of that dark cloud that visits me from time to time.

i named her nyx, after the greek goddess of night. i wanted her to have a beautiful name and i like that she is a powerful goddess reminding me that the darkness is not evil, it is just a place i visit sometimes. i want to honour that she is a part of me... i am both dark and light.

the new job i have given her is to be my guide when i wish to hunt in the shadows and when i need to retreat into my dark cave to rest and reset, to heal, to create, to germinate. her name, nyx, also reminds me that i can be a phoenix... i can RISE and RISE again.

unworthy.

unworthy: not enough of something. too much of something else. not deserving. not special.

this is that feeling that we carry that we are **just not enough.**

this feeling is pervasive. and it happens because we've learned to base our worthiness on our standing in relation to others. we live in a world where we (and the world around us) puts everyone on some type of pedestal. we put others on a pedestal of being more than us, just as we put ourselves on a pedestal when we feel we are more than them.

this is a really dangerous situation we are creating where our worthiness – our enoughness – depends on others. these pedestals are not stable at all... it's impossible to survive for long on a precarious perch based on your placement against others.

it's like you are choosing to play a game of falling dominos... only worse. because it's your self-worth on the line.

and so we must **stop hustling for our worthiness** by striving and trying and waiting to be 'enough' – special enough, good enough, smart enough, whatever enough.

and we must **stop dimming our light** so that others who are *'more worthy'* may shine instead.

what we need to do instead is **claim our worthiness.**

and one way that we can learn to do that is to...

celebrate good times.

celebration is a powerful, powerful mindset tool — and one i think that is often overlooked.

yes, we will celebrate at certain times because it feels appropriate, even fun, but we don't do it to the extent that i want you to do it here. this is about being intentional with celebration, as a practical, purposeful strategy. (not just a once in a while event.)

here's the magic:

when we celebrate our success we train our brains to believe **we are worthy and deserving of success.**

when we celebrate our strengths, our gifts, our talents, our service we train our brains to believe that **what we offer the world has value.**

when we celebrate who we are, as we are, we train our brains to believe that **who we are is actually, perfectly enough.**

and so we celebrate. with intention.

celebrate the evidence that you have amassed over the years of all of the ways that you shine... celebrate those moments of courage, those periods of action taking, those times that you felt guided or on purpose... celebrate the reminders of your inner strength, of your creativity, of your dreams coming true!

the truth is that many of us carry around with us a massive load of evidence of all of our short comings – we carry around the proof of our failures, the moments of rejection, the reminders of everything we can't do and didn't do and aren't doing well – these things stick with us.

we *rarely* carry around the evidence of our success... we might celebrate for a moment but then we move on from that and pick up our heavy 'baggage' once again, baggage that is full of all of the proof of our 'not enoughness'.

we need to give at least equal space to carrying around the evidence of our brilliance... if not more!

this is why:

each moment you celebrate creates a snapshot for your lifetime 'album' of achievement. it's the *whole* album that becomes important (not just those individual pictures of failure or rejection or not good enough).

celebrate your wins, your successes, your achievements and accomplishments. even the very smallest of wins, even the little steps you take along the way. notice more of these moments... and celebrate them!

and remember to amplify your efforts wherever you are at right now.

if you've been celebrating big moments, add in more small ones. if you've been celebrating by quietly patting yourself on the back, start sharing them out loud. (remember your zones of comfort and expand outwards!) there is more power and a greater shift in you when you share your celebration publicly... **you own it by sharing it!**

celebrate your strengths, your talents, your gifts, your zone of genius... celebrate the difference you make and the way that you help people and the way that you are uniquely you. again, own it by sharing it. say out loud: *did you know that one of my special talents is xyz?* or say: *this is the feedback i received today, i am really honoured to help others in this way.*

work on this: **when people tell you they love what you do, believe them!**

just think, when you tell someone that you love what they do, you mean it right? so don't brush it off as luck, as them being nice, or act as if it's no big deal. your light matters, so own that.

practice NOT brushing off compliments, thanks, or kudos. say out loud: *thank you. i am glad to help with that,* or *i am glad to hear that.*

celebrate yourself with more self-love.

you don't have to wait for someone to tell you that you matter — you can speak those words to yourself. you can love yourself with what you say to yourself, with your acts of self-love, even with your awareness. look in the mirror and see all of the ways you are beautiful and strong and unique (rather than your short-comings). practice loving yourself up instead of beating yourself up.

if we want others to think we are worthy, valuable, deserving, enough... we must first think these things of ourselves. we need to engage in radical self-love, we need to celebrate the abundance of not just what we have, and what we do, but of *who we are...* because abundance *is* enoughness.

it's time to believe in your own brilliance. the more you celebrate *you* the more you build that belief in yourself.

we RISE when we claim our worth.

uncertain.

this is the perfect topic to follow on from feeling unworthy. feeling uncertain is a very close cousin, and we need to build up on that worthy evidence that you've been gathering, in order to build:

self-confidence. self-assurance. self-trust. certainty. surety. belief.

a big difference between people who take action towards whatever it is they say they want in the world, and those that don't, is their **belief that they can succeed.**

when we don't feel confident we don't bother — we procrastinate, we avoid, we make excuses — we feel stuck. nothing happens because we do nothing, but we feel like a failure anyways, lowering our confidence even further.

the more confidence we have in ourselves, in our abilities, in our capacity to succeed, the more likely we are to act. the more we act, the more we build evidence of our success. the more evidence we amass, the more confidence we build.

in other words, you can build an upward spiral for yourself or you can stay in the downward one... it's your choice. confidence, like any mindset, is not something that magically appears. we build it!

we start building it with the positive evidence of our worth and our strength and our success... as we mentioned in the 'celebrate' strategy.

now it's time to take that further, because what we need to build is not just confidence in what we have done but confidence in our capacity to do more.

we need to build the **belief**, and even more so, the **certainty** in our potential.

visualising the successful outcome of our actions is a commonly suggested way to build belief in our success. athletes do this by visualizing themselves making the shot, scoring the goal, winning the race. they say that mental visualization is as powerful, if not more powerful, than physical training.

vision boards are also a popular strategy for this reason. when we focus on the successful outcome, the goal, the destination, the object of our dream – as though it is a reality, a done deal – we are more likely to actually achieve that dream.

however, i feel that there is a problem with these types of strategies for many of us: we build in an automatic fail-safe to our dreams.

we visualize the positive outcome but there is still a piece of us whispering: *nothing is certain. it still might not happen. i will try, but just in case i fail, i won't get my hopes up. it would be nice, and i can have big dreams, but i shouldn't count on it* happening. so just in case, i will prepare myself to not get what i want.

here's what i think happens: we are taught to have big dreams. we are taught that we can have whatever we want. we learn about manifesting. we set a goal. we create a vision board. we visualize a positive outcome. and for a moment it is fun, it is exciting, we believe!

but that big goal provokes some big doubt. the seeds of uncertainty get planted and we question our ability to actually succeed. and so begins the downward spiral.

so let's try this: instead of trying to believe in something so big, something you feel very uncertain about, instead start with...

what you know for sure.

...and then build up from there. i call this **the certainty game.**

here's the point of the game: we are going to build certainty, build confidence, build belief in the possibility of our dreams, in the capacity to succeed... by sneaking up on it slowly. when we build it slowly, incrementally, we are less likely to activate the doubt and the fear that will hold us back.

here's how you play:

think of one thing you need to build up your certainty for: the goal you have, the dream, the thing you want to succeed at, the action you need to take.

this big thing is the focus of your game board. but rather than start by visualizing the successful outcome as a 'done deal' (and thus provoking your doubt in your capacity to actually make it happen) we are going to start instead with something more concrete.

start by asking yourself this one question:

what do i know for sure?

you have evidence of your success, your strengths, your gifts, your talents, your abilities, your impact. we gathered that evidence in the celebrate strategy.

so start with one thing that you know for sure.

that one thing holds the first place of your game board. from there i want you to move to the next spot by asking:

if that is true, and i know that it is, what else could also be true?

for example, if you know that you have helped one other person, is it also possible that you could help more than one?

if you know you have done something similar before, is it also possible that you could do it again in this instance?

you then move to the next spot on the game board by asking:

and if so, then what?

and keep asking: **then what?**

with each step on the game board add to the question of what is possible, based on what you already know for sure. keep going until you get closer and closer to that big dream or big goal.

your game board might end up looking like more of a mind map than a linear pathway... and that's ok! it might also look a bit like a snakes and ladders game board.

if you get to a spot where your inner dragon says: "ha! that's never going to happen! because you suck! you might find yourself sliding down the snake back to the beginning. that's ok too... just go back to your question: "what do i know for sure?" – and build up your belief and your confidence again from that place.

when you get back to that snake – that inner dragon – you can be ready to respond from a place of strength... use your answer of what you know for sure to respond to that voice before the dragon even has a chance to strike, no more sliding back down again!

the key is: **start with what you know for sure and build up from there.**

build your certainty, build your confidence, build your belief, build your trust in you.

we RISE when we believe we can.

crickets.

do you know the feeling?

you share something, you say something, you do something... something that you believe matters... and *nothing*.

no comments. no replies. no engagement. no traction. no impact. no thanks. no recognition. no response.

crickets.

it can be such a discouraging feeling, can't it?

you might start getting a case of the 'why bothers'. you might start questioning your words, your ideas, your work. you might even feel like giving up.

i get it. i've been there too.

but remember this... this quote from anne lamott[6] that inspired the lighthouse revolution: *lighthouses don't go running all over an island looking for boats to save; they just stand there shining.*

that's the whole point.

you have to be the lighthouse.

you have to **act as if**... as if there are 1000 boats, or 100 boats, or even just *one* boat out there, lost at sea, needing your light.

focus on ONE boat.

close your eyes. picture that one person out there... that one reader. that one listener. that one viewer. that one stranger. that one future friend. that one like-minded soul.

what do they need to hear today?

- → you are not alone.
- → it's going to be ok.
- → you've got this.

speak to them. talk directly to that one person. act as if they are already out there... waiting, searching, listening... show up for them.

and show up again. and again.

this little trick works when you are trying to overcome your own fear to try something new: to share something vulnerable on social media; to do your first facebook live, podcast, or blog post; to write a book; to send a letter to your community, speak up in a meeting, or walk over and talk to that group of people.

it can be hard to overcome our own resistance, that voice in our head saying: *who am i to do this? what if people don't like it? what if all i get is crickets?*

we need a reason to show up and shine... let that one boat out at sea be your reason. focus on them.

talk to them. shine out your light to them. act as if they are already there waiting for you.

this helps too if you are writing an article for someone else's blog or website, speaking to someone in a podcast or interview, attempting to be published in a magazine or a collaborative book, even speaking up in a group forum or a at a community event. it can be hard to know what to say... what will appeal to someone else's audience. instead, just picture your one boat out there at sea. talk to them. write for them.

the keeper of the beacon is the rockstar. to build up your resilience and overcome your resistance you need to tap into your inner rockstar... rock star energy is about standing, authentically, on your own kind of stage, singing out the song of your soul.

what would that mean to you? it doesn't have to mean actually standing on a stage! it could be more like standing out on a street corner like an indie rocker playing to the beat of your own drum. or maybe it's hanging up your work in a gallery, or adding it to the shelves of a library, or standing at the front of a classroom, or showing off your stuff in the pages of a magazine, or speaking up at meetings!

start *acting as if* right now. let your blog, your video, your email, your facebook, your instagram be that stage... and share yourself as though your audience, your boats, are out there *already waiting for you.*

here's the thing we forget sometimes.

everybody starts at zero.

every single person you admire for shining their light in the world started at zero.

but it's the people who keep showing up, keep RISING up, keep trying, keep tweaking... keep shining... that *grow* from zero.

it requires tenacity, perseverance, resilience... grit... to build that up in yourself, to ignore the crickets, to focus on your one boat out at sea... and act as if you are already the lighthouse.

meh.

dejected. discouraged. dispirited.

give up mode.

call it what you want. i like the word 'meh'... it sounds like it feels.

maybe you've had a disappointment. maybe you are feeling low. maybe you've lost your direction, lost your clarity, lost your way. maybe you are questioning everything, wondering why bother? who cares? what's the point?

when i feel like this i just want to retreat. i want to hide in my bed. and i often just want to wait for some magical moment where things shift or the epiphany comes.

but the truth is, for that moment of shift or epiphany or for things to lighten up and feel better... you've got to meet the universe half way.

nothing will change if you hide in your bed. **if you want something different to happen you have to do something different.**

but what do you do, how can you take action when you are feeling so lost or down?

show up and help someone.

set yourself that one simple task... just show up and help someone today.

even if you'd rather just keep hiding in your bed... pop your head out, even for just 15 minutes, and help someone else. do this for 3 days. and then for 10 days. and then 21 days. just keep doing it... no other agenda but just showing up and helping someone. every day.

notice what happens. notice how you feel. notice what shifts. notice what unfolds... when you focus not on your *own* stuckness but rather on helping someone else out of *theirs*.

i do know that can feel overwhelming at times.

the world needs changing. there is no doubt about that. some days it really feels like it's all too big to fix, it's all so hard, where do we even begin?

and in light of the big problems of the world that can overwhelm us, the work we do do might seem insignificant, frivolous even.

but i am reminded of this quote from mr. rogers[7]: *when i was a boy and i would see scary things in the news, my mother would say to me, 'look for the helpers. you will always find people who are helping.' to this day, especially in times of disaster, i remember my mother's words, and i am always comforted by realizing that there are still so many helpers — so many caring people in this world.*

be a helper... just show up and help someone today.

don't think about how insignificant your thing feels... remember how important it is to *help someone* with your thing. focus on how you help people.

the other thing to remember is that in order to change the world we must first change ourselves. the work starts within.

so anything that you offer to someone that helps them be the person they are here to be, that helps them to shine brighter in the world, that helps them heal or shift or grow or evolve or get ignited, that helps them to RISE up and speak out and teach and share and help someone else... well that matters.

and an interesting thing often happens when we reach out to help others. what you feel called to teach or share is often the very thing that you yourself need to learn or remember. **helping someone else just might be a clue as to what will help you too!**

if you are feeling lost, frustrated, confused, uncertain, scared, helpless, questioning, sad, angry, dispirited...

just show up and help someone today. see what happens.

we RISE when we lift others.

failure.

it is so important to celebrate your successes, achievements, and wins. not only is it important to keep your light ignited and your vibes high... but as we now know, it is also an important mindset strategy. celebrating success trains your brain to believe that you are worthy and deserving of success.

but what do you do about all of the failures?

what do you do about that list of things that didn't work out or didn't go well or didn't get anywhere... those dreams you started out with that fizzled or flopped?

sometimes even all the success in the world can't take away the pain of the one thing you failed at or fucked up.

here's what i am learning to do to as a strategy to deal with failure.

give everything you do, try, share, offer, or explore...

a new purpose.

there is always the **obvious purpose**... for instance if you've created something to sell you have the purpose of earning money. if you've created a freebie to give away you have the purpose of building your community. if you've filmed a youtube video you have the purpose of people watching that video. if you've signed up for a course to learn something you have the purpose of becoming good at it. you're probably tracking your sales, your list size, your views and likes, your grades.

but what i am noticing is that if that obvious purpose is the *only* purpose it is so very easy to feel like you've failed if you don't meet that goal.

it can help if we give our efforts a **grander purpose** than the obvious one.

if you have created something... what could be a purpose that means even more to you than sales or likes?

perhaps the thing you create has the purpose of reminding people about your zone of genius, what you can help them with, or the difference you can make. perhaps you would simply like to see if it resonates. perhaps you can practice selling your thing so that it feels authentic and fun and aligned. perhaps you can push out of your comfort zone, sharing with new people in new places. perhaps you wish to simply give yourself the space to be creative, to brainstorm, to try out new things.

if you are learning or trying something new, perhaps you could make it less about how good you are (your grade or other sign of achievement) and instead make your purpose to explore how it feels to you.

does it feel fun? interesting? like you want to keep working at it? or does it feel boring or like it's maybe not your thing?

if you have a fresh new idea to present or a view point you want to share, perhaps it isn't about how many people jump on board or agree with you, but rather it's an opportunity to build your confidence in speaking up or your comfort with standing out. the measure of success then becomes the act of speaking up, not the success of the idea itself.

if you can give what you do a meaningful purpose beyond the obvious then you will still have accomplished so much even if you don't make any sales, or get the top marks, or whatever else was the obvious purpose.

one of my strengths is creating things and getting them out there. i am pretty good at overcoming my fear and my need for perfection, which means that i am good at taking action and taking the leap and just making shit happen.

but my challenge is that if the stuff i create/ share/ offer 'flops' i feel like i have failed... it knocks me right down, and i can get stuck in a discouraged place... this old story of *'nothing ever lands'* and *'maybe i should just give up.'*

the way i am trying to shift that pattern it is to give my efforts a grander purpose. something that can't flop: something like learning or noticing or exploring or testing or practicing or stretching.

that way, no matter what happens, it's still a win... there is still something to celebrate.

don't get me wrong. a failure still hurts. it's hard not to meet your goal.

i think back to the kickstarter for my first book <u>lighthouse revolution</u>. i am so very grateful to the 140 backers who made it such a huge success... and i am really proud of myself too. but what if i had failed? what if i hadn't met my goal? it would have hit me hard, i know it, i wouldn't feel proud of myself for having given it a go, i would just feel like a failure.

that's why i want to shift that pattern. i don't want to put myself in a position where everything hinges on one certain outcome.

when i did my second kickstarter for the illuminate oracle deck, i approached it with a different mindset. i created a meaningful purpose beyond the obvious crowdfunding goal — i set myself a challenge of helping someone every day. i set myself a goal of reaching out to new people that i otherwise never would have talked to. and i set myself a goal of showing up and giving it my absolute best shot every day.

if i didn't reach my goal — if i had gotten a big red F in raising the funds for my project — i still would have given myself a B+ for my side goal of helping people and an A+ for showing up every day with my best effort. when i did reach my goal i celebrated all of my successes, but i also asked: what could i do better? i gave myself a C- for creativity, so that can be a new purpose for my next launch... can i find some creative ways to share my thing and help people... be a little more inventive and fun!

giving the things you do a new purpose isn't a strategy for 'dealing with failure' — it's about finding ways to make failure not even a thing to deal with any more... to **find the successes in every effort.** and to let those successes — even the small ones — be the foundation blocks we keep building on instead of letting so-called failures become wrecking balls that knock us down.

we RISE even when we fail.

annoyed & irritated.

i am sure you know this feeling, we've all been there! it can happen when you feel like someone...

- takes advantage of you
- asks too much of you
- doesn't respect you
- disregards you
- puts you in an uncomfortable spot
- takes and takes but never gives back

it can also happen when you are irritated with yourself! you feel like you...

- are dropping balls
- not following through
- not honouring yourself
- not doing what you need to be doing
- have no time, no energy, no focus for the stuff that matters

when these feelings come up... when you feel supper annoyed or irritated with someone else or with yourself or even with your circumstances... it's a sign: it's time to create some new boundaries and systems or to tighten up existing ones.

it is important to have a good understanding of what boundaries actually are.

boundaries are not walls that divide you, they are not barriers that constrain you... they are simply how you honour yourself (your time, your energy, your feelings, your needs, your focus) and how you decide for yourself as well as teach others: **this is what is ok.**

the best boundaries are for *ideas* — the things that cause your irritation such as fear, doubt, lack, criticism, judgement, control — not for *people*. in other words, you don't have to say to someone: *you can't come here, i don't have time for you, you are not ok.* instead you say: *that sort of shame and judgement can't come here, i don't have time for gossip and criticism, those demands are not ok.*

a great way to have a look at your boundaries and the way things are running in your life is to...

hire an assistant.

ok, not really. i know you can't hire an assistant just like that. but for this strategy pretend like you are! *act* like you are hiring a personal assistant, a virtual assistant, a secretary, an employee, a minion... someone besides *you* who can get shit done, and not be so attached emotionally!

just have a think about it: if you had an assistant...

→ they would say yes/no to people and things based on your criteria, without feeling bad about it
→ they would protect your time
→ they would enforce your boundaries

→ and they would honour your systems and structures...

...because you are paying them to make your life easier! right?

if you were hiring an assistant you would have to outline everything for them...

- everything you say yes or no to
- what you will spend time on and what you won't
- what is ok and what is not ok
- what to say when you get asked certain things or get treated in a certain way
- what jobs need to be done, what steps to take, and how
- how much time things should take
- what is allowed in your space and what is not

you don't want to pay them to take too much time, and you don't want them to make mistakes! so write it all down. create the 'owner's manual' for running the vehicle of YOU.

create boundaries: *this is what is ok, and this is what is not ok.*

create systems: *when this happens i will do this.*

prepare responses: *when i get asked to do this, this is what i say.*

and remember that the stuff that has been annoying and irritating you, it's all just another clue or sign...

be grateful for it when it shows up! *"thank you person/situation for showing me what i need to tighten up, what i need to clarify... before it happens again!"*

a few fabulous things happen when we act like we are hiring an assistant and create the 'owner's manual' for our lives... when we write out our boundaries and our systems.

once we put those things down on the page they become **less of a thing we struggle with and more just something we do** – it takes some of the emotion out of it! our brain goes: *well this is what it says in the manual, so this is what we do!*

we also tend to honour what we have written down. rather than wondering what to do, and rather than doing it sometimes but not others, once we write it down it becomes this official sort of thing... we just *know* what to do or say.

it also helps us to honour our time. if you wouldn't pay an assistant to take hours to do that thing – write that email reply or do that job or deal with that situation – then why would we let ourselves take hours?!

when you sit down to do the jobs on your list you can actually act like you *are* the assistant. just get 'r done! you can even reply to that pesky email like you are your assistant. you can give your imaginary assistant a name and persona and then put on their hat when you sit down to do the job.

the next time you find yourself in a situation where you are feeling irritated or annoyed with someone — or yourself — just ask: what is this situation showing me? where do i need to create or tighten up my boundaries or systems? something clearly isn't working for me, so i need to make some adjustments.

open up the 'owner's manual' for your life and keep working on it!

the work is never really done — your boundaries will shift and change just as you do, your systems will need to be tweaked — but you are always the boss of you. you decide what is ok and what is not ok, and then you teach yourself or others what you are going to about it do from now on!

self-sabotage.

i think everyone deals with self-sabotage at some point.

the reason that we subconsciously sabotage ourselves is because we each have an **upper limit problem** – a subconscious upper limit of what feels good and what goes well and what we can have; an upper limit of succuss, achievement, love, abundance, creativity, and joy.

picture it like a thermostat: when we dial up or make a leap into what feels good, we hit our upper limit and activate the thermostat... we set off the limiting beliefs and old bullshit stories that we have been carrying around for a long time.

uh oh! this is too good. if i shine bright something bad is going to happen! because: i am not good enough, i am abandoning who i was and where i came from, i can't possibly outshine others, i will lose everything, i will totally screw this up... success is a burden that i can't handle.

this is what happens: we dial up our light, we shine bright – we stretch, we expand, we leap, we RISE – and then we sabotage ourselves in order to *protect* ourselves, to *punish* ourselves, or to *prevent* anything bad from happening. and so we go back to being small, same, safe, stuck.

self-sabotage can look like this:

- getting sick or hurt
- screwing up, making mistakes
- reneging on commitments, breaking promises
- retreating, hiding, avoiding, quitting
- creating drama, arguments, blaming others

it's important to recognize both your **limiting beliefs**: those fears that prevent you from shining your light, and your **personal sabotages**: the ways you protect or punish yourself. as you have more awareness of what is actually going on in your situation you will have a better capacity to shift out of this place and keep shining!

one way to dissolve the limiting belief and pattern of self-sabotage is to build up a sense of safety... you need to feel incredibly safe to shine: to feel good, to take action, to have more of what you say you want, to RISE.

when you notice your own self-sabotage...

build a safety net.

first, ask yourself: **what would it take to feel safe?** make a list. for example:

- have more support around me
- get clear on my responsibilities and obligations
- have a plan to deal with any backlash or criticism
- have a plan B and a plan C in case things change

next, build up your sense of safety in your current situation by using this phrase: **it is safe to____**. for example:

- it is safe to take this step
- it is safe to have everything i want
- it is safe to feel this good
- it is safe to make progress

and then look around you and follow up with: **because____**. this add on will help you anchor into that feeling of safety even more. for example:

- because i am so ready, i have done all of the preparation, done the ground work
- because i have the support of my team, my mentors, my peers
- because i collected the evidence that proves i am good at this
- because i am ready with a plan b if this doesn't work
- because i know exactly how to respond if someone says xyz

keep working on your list until you begin to feel a little ridiculous for even being worried in the first place or until the safety feels stupidly obvious, like: *duh! of course it's safe!*

my most common self-sabotage is getting sick... as soon as i start RISING or shining, i will get a cold or a sore throat or a sinus infection and need to retreat to my bed. i have also noticed that if i am not feeling very mentally or emotionally strong then physically i will begin to feel run down... it is as though my body is giving me a 'good' reason to stay small and safe in bed.

i am trying now to be more specific and truthful about how i feel. instead of saying *"i am not feeling well, i am staying home"* i will try something like *"i am feeling sad today, i need some time to myself."* i don't want the excuse of "i am not feeling well" to become a self-fulfilling prophecy, getting physically sick every time i feel down mentally or emotionally!

i have also gotten much better at recognising this run down feeling in my body that precedes getting sick. when i notice it i check in: in what way am i pushing my upper limit buttons? and i give myself a day to rest, to 'shore up' and recalibrate. i will say to myself: *thank you body for protecting me. for giving me a moment to strengthen up for my next steps. it is safe for me to move forwards now, it is safe for me to RISE.*

you might choose a few of your best "it's safe to..." statements to use as a mantra; **speaking out loud can help you own the truth of your safety.**

you might need to make your safety list over and over again, daily even, to completely dissolve the sabotage... but that is ok! this practice is actually really important, so do it often!

when you do this exercise you begin to **train your brain to notice how safe you are rather than the danger you are in** (everything you ought to be afraid of, worried about, or feel bad about).

this is a great 'new job' for that inner dragon who is notorious for finding and reacting to danger... get him noticing where is safe instead!

we RISE when we feel safe and supported.

***

play more: read <u>the big leap</u> by gay hendricks for more on the upper limit problem, limiting beliefs, and self-sabotage.

worry.

worry. that whisper, that voice, that says:

what if something bad happens. what if i fail. what if everyone hates it. what if everyone hates me. what if everything goes wrong. what if i can't handle it. what if everything works out. what if everything changes now.

what if.

a big reason we listen to the voice of the worry (and fear and doubt and limiting belief) that whispers in our mind is that we are very busy dwelling in either the past or in the future. we carry around those old bullshit stories from the past or we create new bullshit stories based on what might happen in the future.

it is not the best place to be when you are trying to take positive action in the here and now. instead you need to...

be where your feet are.

just think of that phrase for a moment: *be where your feet are.*

you are trying to take action, to take steps forward, right here right now... yet your mind, your thoughts, your beliefs, your emotions, your energy is stuck back in the past or ahead in the future.

doesn't it make more sense to be where your feet are? to be in the here and now, in the present?

this is something we actually have to practice to get better at.

most of the strategies we have already mentioned will help you to be more present in the here and now – the *safety net* does this, so does the *certainty game* when we start with what we know for sure, so does *celebrating*, and so does *helping someone else* and having an *anchor*.

all of these things help to get you into the present moment because you focus on what you can do or what it means for you **right here, right now.**

and all of those strategies help us to deal with a kind of stuckness that is based on future tripping or past dwelling – carrying the weight of old stuff or fearing the stuff that might happen.

you can also do some mindfulness activities to help bring you into the present, at any time, in any situation... whenever you realize you are not being where your feet are!

try:

focusing on your breath.

mindful breathing is a very simple yet powerful tool for getting out of your head, or out of some big emotions or energy, and being more present in the body and present in the moment. a simple breathing technique you can try anywhere, anytime is 'square breathing' – breathe in for 4 counts, hold for 4, breathe out for 4 counts, hold for 4, and repeat a number of times. you can even draw a square with your finger as you do it for added focus. (this is an easy technique to teach to children as well!)

focusing on your awareness.

when we are busy dwelling in the past or future – when we are stuck in thoughts, emotions, worries etc. – we are not very aware of the here and now. you would have noticed this if you've ever ended up in your car at your destination and realized you don't really remember the trip! a simple mindfulness strategy is to notice what is around you, in the here and now... it brings you right back into the present and into your true self. just pause and list 10 things that you sense: i see blue sky, i hear a bird, i see a red car over there, i smell the sea air, etc.

focusing on your body.

similar to breath and awareness, we can focus on our physical body. feel the ground beneath your feet, the steering wheel in your hands, the way your waistband is rubbing your side, the way the soft fabric of your t-shirt feels on your skin. you can also do a physical activity to get more focused on your body – i find that yoga gets me out of my head and into my body like nothing else, but you might try running or jumping or dancing or walking out on the grass. try to focus on getting into your body rather than getting lost in your thoughts.

focusing on an activity.

colouring is a perfect example of this and of course mindful colouring books have become all the rage. you get to focus on something in the here and now and let your brain rest for a while. i find that knitting or crochet does this for me really well and you might have other activities that do it for you... house cleaning perhaps? playing a musical instrument? anything that helps you to get into the present moment with a physical task that you focus on.

focus on an object.

this is a similar idea to having an anchor, a touchstone, or talisman that you can hang on to... let a physical object be your touchstone to bring you back to the present. snap an elastic on your wrist, twist your ring, hold onto a pendant around your neck, put a crystal or a rock in your pocket to hold. as you do, be mindful about it, be intentional. what do you want that touchstone to remind you of? you might even attach a short mantra to it: 'it is safe to...' 'one thing i know for sure...' 'i am ready...'

the more you practice mindfulness the easier all of the other strategies in this book will become as well, because in order for them to work we need to stop letting the fears, worries, doubts, frustrations, etc – which are based on stuff that happened in the past or might happen in the future – be the boss of us.

in order to get unstuck from that stuff we need to be where our feet are, focused on the present moment... we need to listen to the wise voice of our best self, and take steps in the here and now.

***

play more: the little book of still by annie harvey has some wonderful, simple ideas for mindfulness.

overwhelm.

i am sure you have felt this feeling of overwhelm:

oh my god there is so much to do and not enough time and where do i even start and what if i can't do it all and what if i can't handle all of this...

it's like a little ball of 'to do' list gets mixed in with worry and starts to spin and build and snowball and turns into massive overwhelm with some extra panic and stress thrown in.

yuck.

overwhelm can happen in part from the future tripping and past dwelling we just talked about — worry, doubt, and fear will add to that giant to do list in your mind — so the mindfulness activities to help you be where your feet are will definitely help.

overwhelm can also happen when life gets busy, when we are not protecting our boundaries, when we don't have helpful systems, and when we spend our currency (time, energy, focus) in the wrong places.

and overwhelm can happen whenever we decide to take a leap, to RISE up or to expand in some way... to shine. even when we feel excited about something we can also self-sabotage ourselves with overwhelm.

the most important thing is to not let overwhelm be a barrier to taking action... don't let it stop you in your tracks. instead give it a new job – let it be a clue for you.

is this feeling of overwhelm pointing to some inner work you need to do? for instance: feeling safe, training your inner dragon, or building your self-belief?

once you recognize what else might be going on you can get back to the task at hand and deal with the pressure building in that spinning snowball!

start with a big brain dump.

get all of that stuff that is adding to that feeling of overwhelm out of your head and down on the page. if you don't, it just keeps spinning and spinning up there, growing in force like a tornado... you need to let it out. thinking about it doesn't work, it just keeps spinning. you need to open the valve and let it pour out... write it out, or speak it out to someone if that is more effective for you.

you might need to brain dump over and over and over again, even with the same list of stuff. and that is ok. it doesn't always work to do it just once and then move on... keep brain dumping if you need to! keep a notebook beside your bed just in case you need to do this before you sleep at night... spinning overwhelm can be a terrible culprit preventing you from falling asleep!

once you brain dump, you have only one job...

choose ONE thing.

that's it. **one thing.** choose and focus on your one thing from that wild brain dump... the rest you leave for another day. what one thing do you focus on? try <u>one</u> of these...

- → **choose your priority.** start with the most important thing right now, the rest can wait
- → **follow your purpose.** whatever ignites you and excites you, whatever is within your zone of genius, whatever you are most passionate about
- → **start with the easiest, funnest thing.** we often make things harder than they need to be! try asking yourself: what would be the easiest, funnest thing? do that!
- → **choose the next best step.** we don't have to have it all figured out, mapped out, we can just go with what seems like the next best step and go from there.

know this: you cannot do this *wrong*. whatever you choose as your one thing, you will build momentum from there, and the next steps will appear.

the truth is that all anyone can ever do is take one step at a time... one foot in front of the other... left, right, left, right... like a march... until we get it all done. we start with one step, then we take another, and another.

and it *will* all get done. that's the thing we often forget when we are in the state of overwhelm, it puts us in a place of disbelief and worry and doubt. but the reality is that no matter how much there is to do, it will eventually all be done.

just pause for a moment and picture that future moment – when it is all said and done, when it's finished or it has happened or it is all a success or even simply when this big list of jobs has been completed.

picture *that*. anchor into that feeling: *you're done. you've done it.*

and with that picture in mind, that knowing that it *will* in fact all be done, trust in that. when the overwhelm hits you can tell that voice in your head: *it's ok, it will all get done. right now i will focus on my one thing. and i will keep marching on from there.*

i often tell myself this: *the time will pass anyways! wouldn't i rather be done all of this then? wouldn't i rather be where i want to be? rather than still spinning exactly where i am right now?*

if the time will pass anyways i would rather be taking steps forward than still stuck where i am.

just start with one thing. march on from there.

disconnected.

untethered. uninspired. adrift. unguided.

for this strategy we are talking about feeling disconnected from your soul, from your intuition, from a higher purpose, from the universe... having no faith or trust, not feeling guided, no real belief in anything.

it might seem like a strange feeling to include here... why does this count as feeling stuck?

it might not, for you, at first glance. you might be thinking your personal brand of stuckness has nothing to do with feeling disconnected from faith or soul... maybe this is not even something you've ever really even considered in your life... but this feeling can in fact add layers to anything you are experiencing right now.

and shifting it – feeling connected again – can make a difference to everything.

you can think of it any way you like:

→ a connection to something **inside** of you, like your intuition, your soul, your inner light or inner knowing;
→ a connection to something **outside** of you, like your guides or angels;
→ a connection to something **bigger** than you, like god, source, spirit, or divine.

whatever you want to call it, however you want to define it, it's all the same. here's how i think of it: we have a light inside of us, the light of our soul. we can connect to our own inner light, our intuition, and we can connect to the source of that light, the source of all light, something outside of us... a divine light.

what i have noticed is that having some sort of connection to soul and connection to spirit does indeed make a difference when you are trying to RISE... call it a spiritual practice, call it listening to your gut, call it whatever you like. define it your way. do it your way.

feeling connected helps you to remember your inherent worthiness, it helps you to take action, it helps you to listen to that voice of real you or lighthouse you, it helps you to have purpose, it helps you to be courageous and expand your comfort zone... all of the things we have been talking about in this book!

every kind of stuckness that you can possibly experience will have fear at the core, if you peel away enough layers. fear is what limits us, what constrains us... it's what creates worry and doubt and frustration and lack.

the way through all fear is love.

a course in miracles[8] states: *if you knew who walked beside you on the path that you have chosen, fear would be impossible.*

when you have faith and trust, when you feel connected to your soul and connected to something beyond yourself — the source of all light — you connect into pure love.

if you can begin to believe that you *are* light, and that you are a vehicle for light to work through you, then who are you NOT to shine?

fear comes from the ego, love comes from the soul. so what we want to do here is practice connecting to our soul. (source, spirit, universe, light. you get the idea... you call it what you want.) we are going to do this by going on a...

treasure hunt.

yep, i want you to act like a pirate! it's maybe not the most 'spiritual' image to bring to mind, but i have done this on purpose because i want this to be fun — i want you to smile, to laugh, to feel a bit playful — there is no better way to tap into the high vibe energy of light than to have fun!

so we are going to act like a pirate and search for treasure.

start by thinking about the road so far... where you've been and what you've experienced. you can think of that – the journey you have been on – as part of your treasure map. as you look back on that road, where are the moments that you:

- trusted your intuition or felt it and did not trust it
- felt guided or called or like you had a higher purpose
- felt the most faith and trust, and the least
- noticed signs, messages, nudges

think back and explore your memories, search through them, **look for buried treasure.** you are looking for anything that offers a clue to what connection looks like, feels like, and sounds like to *you.*

you might also notice some things to heal, release, or clear. maybe moments you could forgive yourself or others, maybe moments that you could learn from and then let go. you have strategies in your toolbelt for that now!

next we are going to **explore the here and now.**

→ *how do you think your intuition works?* you might feel something in your body, you might see things in your mind's eye or see things popping up around you, you might hear things or notice words around you, you might just have a strong sense of knowing.

→ *how do you feel most connected to your inner light or to divine light?* do you feel it when you walk at the beach or stand in the shower or sit in the grass? do you go to church? do you pray or meditate or have another spiritual practice? do you use oracle cards?

→ *how do you feel guided?* perhaps you see signs around you (repeating numbers, feathers), perhaps you notice people or messages popping into your life, perhaps you get goosebumps or tingles on your head or butterflies in your tummy. perhaps you have strange dreams, or get messages through music, or notice animals around you.

for any of these areas, remember that there is no right or wrong way to feel connected. you are on a treasure hunt, looking for clues in your own daily life. these little clues are points on the treasure map, pointing you towards strengthening your connection.

i had a big AHA when i did a friend's online quiz on psychic connection and learned something about how connection works for me via words, phrases, quotes, and music lyrics. suddenly the notebooks full of lyrics and quotes that i had collected from the time i was young made sense to me! since finding that little bit of treasure, i get messages all of the time through music... it was like my switch turned on.

during my period of grief and 'shut down' i took a break from music... i just wasn't ready for whatever it had to say. shortly after my dad died, i went down to the beach to have my own little good bye. as i sat alone on a secluded little part of the beach, music started playing! a group of young people were down in the water swimming and had a speaker blasting on the shore. the song was 'so happy together' and i burst into tears... my parents were sending me a beautiful message.

as soon as i got the message, before the song was even over, the music changed. one after another i received song after song, message after message, from my parents. it was a beautiful affirmation that they are always with me, always loving me. the final song came on the car radio as i drove home... 'love shack' which was one of our favourite back yard, pool party, karaoke songs. i felt that my parents were telling me that it was time now to focus on the present... on creating a happy life and our own back yard oasis with our found family here in australia.

even as i share this story now, i am reminded of how profound and amazing that moment on the beach was. i didn't think i was ready for music messages or for feeling all of the feelings, but the music found its way to me regardless. and because i know how connection works for me, the message was received.

when you know how connection works for you, you can play in that space. you can practice, you can notice, and you can say: *thank you! yes yes, more like that please!*

that is the final step of our treasure hunt... from this moment forward, don't just search for treasure, but actually **design the map.**

grab a notebook or journal, perhaps a small one that you can keep in your handbag or pocket or beside your bed. and whenever you have a moment of connection you write it down in your book, you mark the spot on your map.

track your intuition, track the signs and messages, track the feelings and nudges, track the people who show up and say things, track the moments that you feel guided, called, or like you are living in a moment of your soul's purpose... track anything at all that feels like connection.

as you keep track you are creating the map to your treasure: knowing what works for you and how you work. the more you notice the more you will keep noticing – strengthening not just your connection, but also your faith and trust and belief in that connection.

the treasure is in you right now, it is all around you, all you need to do is open your eyes to it.

we RISE when we feel connected and guided.

***

play more: to learn more about how your particular brand of intuition works, try denise litchfield's quiz on psychic strengths at deniselitchfield.com

insignificant.

one reason i have enjoyed talking about the lighthouse over the past few years is that it offers such a great visual about what it is like to RISE up and shine our light.

every lighthouse is needed, yet no two are alike! our significance comes not from how tall we are, from where we are located, or even from how bright our light is... we are significant simply because we shine. we shine for that one boat out there that needs our light.

but, as we have said in this book, it isn't enough to know that we are here to shine, or even to ignite our light within, there is more work to be done. we need to clear those foggy windows, we need to build ourselves up, we need to do the inner work to keep shining and RISING.

and that can start to feel a little all consuming.

we get kind of wrapped up in ourselves, in our stuff.

i once heard gabrielle bernstein[9] talk about this; she said that she was all wrapped up in her own stuff and her friend said this to her: *this is not your business. this is god's business. you are a servant of something fucking unstoppable.*

in other words: get over yourself! this is not about you, this is bigger than you. so just show up and shine.

how do we do that? we must remember that...

we've got work to do.

this phrase is another great line from my favourite tv show, _supernatural_. the two main characters are brothers who fight monsters, demons, and ghosts. when everyone else is running away from the danger, they are running in. no matter how tired, hurt, or broken they are, they show up again and again to help others; they throw their weapons in the trunk of their awesome, classic car and slam the lid shut with a simple phrase: **we've got work to do.**

this line reminds me (and i hope it reminds you too): **this is not all about you.**

no matter what is going on within you, sometimes you just have to get over yourself and show up anyhow, because we've got work to do.

in order for this phrase to work you need to know what that _work_ is.

think about this: _what are you a part of that is bigger than you?_

i know that contemplating your answer to this question — a question about your purpose, your calling, or your work – actually might provoke more stuck stuff: your inner dragon gets loud, you hit your upper limit of what feels possible, you want to hide.

but this is what you need to remember: whatever it is that you are a part of – this bigger work that we are here to do, the work that is bigger than you alone – i am *not* saying that you need to be some sort of guru. this isn't about you changing the whole world. this isn't about being the expert or the leader or the 'face' of anything.

this is about you showing up and adding your voice to the conversation. this is about you being one of the helpers, one of the contributors, one of the supporters of whatever it is that *matters to you*.

i like to think of it like this: the universe has an enormous library, a catalogue of *stuff that matters*, and when you show up and shine – with your words, your actions, your service, your support, your passion, your talent, your art – with the work you do, or the way you live your life, or the way you help people – then you are simply *adding your book* to the shelves of that library.

that's it. **you are adding something to whatever it is that *matters*...** a piece of the puzzle, one that wasn't there before.

so what is it for you? what conversation are you adding to? what book do you add to the shelves?

what is the bigger picture that you are working on here?

and who are the other people who are doing work in this space? who do you admire, respect, follow... who inspires you? like those monster-hunting brothers of my show... who are those people in *your* world?

when we tap into what matters, and who else is showing up and shining in that space, we can remember that there is indeed *still work to do*. those people show up, and so should you, even if it is most simply by the way you live your life or by the way you are changing your own little world.

we RISE when we make a contribution.

shame.

of all of the things that could be hidden away in our darkness, i think that shame might be the one that festers the most and the deepest. when we peel away the layers of whatever stuckness we feel, we just might find shame deep below the surface... and there it grows with secrecy and silence.

the very thing we most *need* to do – to bring that shame to the surface so that it can heal – is the very thing we most *don't want* to do. ironically, we are ashamed of our shame.

shame is the feeling – the deep belief – that: *i am bad*.

it is important to note that this is not quite the same as guilt.

guilt is: i *did* something bad. i made a mistake. guilt is directed towards a behaviour.

shame is directed at the self, at the core of who we are: i *am* something bad. i *am* a mistake.

no wonder that shame leads to fear, doubt, worry, lack, frustration. we believe that we are 'bad' and therefore we are not deserving, we are not capable, we are not confident.

guilt is actually a pretty useful sort of stuckness to feel – you can quite easily give guilt the new job of showing you what you need to do differently. when we feel guilt – *i did something bad* – we can do better, we can repair the damage, we can be sorry, and we can forgive ourselves.

with guilt, the inner healing and clearing actually comes from working on the outward behaviour; we heal our guilt when we fix what we are feeling guilty about. and this is really important work... if we don't do the work on our guilt – on the mistake we made – we can begin to internalize it more and more: '*i made a mistake*' slowly becomes '*i am a mistake*' if we let it all fester in the darkness.

so first and foremost, when you experience that feeling of guilt... do the work! what is that guilt showing you: what do you need to explore? is there a behaviour that you need to adjust? is there some damage you need to repair? is there something that needs to change? where do you need to speak up and own your mistakes? where do you need to take action?

or perhaps you are feeling a guilt that is unwarranted? we can feel guilty when we believe that we aren't doing enough, or aren't good enough, or always screwing up... but it could be that this stuff is not even true! it could be that we haven't actually made a mistake, we are just being hard on ourselves our listening to that lying voice inside. it could point to doing some work we need to do on unworthiness, failure, even overwhelm.

this inner work of healing and repairing and moving on from guilt really is so important. otherwise, the mistakes we make, the imperfections we perceive, the evidence of our shortcomings and failures... we end up carrying this stuff around with us, and it seeps into our soul.

when we beat ourselves up, especially in the long term, it is like saying over and over to our inner selves: 'shame on me. i am bad. i am a mistake.'

so instead of beating yourself up, i want you to...

love yourself up.

you do this when you do the work to build your self-worth and self-confidence, when you listen to the voice of real you and when you connect to your inner light... these are all acts of loving yourself up.

let's be even more intentional. let's give ourselves an absolute shower of compassion! compassion is the most powerful tool in our toolbox to release shame.

start by shining your light of awareness on your shame. this might be harder than any other awareness you have done... shame wants desperately to stay in the dark, so we avoid our shame more than any other shadow in the darkness.

when you whisper those words in your head: *i am bad. i am a mistake. i am broken. i am defective. i am a disappointment. i am wrong.*

what whispers back? where is that shame you carry?

bring it up to the surface... to heal it we need to see it. what is the shame story that has been festering inside of you?

once you have an idea of what you want to focus on, do a visualisation. remember that inner child that you met early on in this book? picture them in your mind's eye. picture them small, cowering, burdened with the weight of that shame. picture a large, imposing, adult figure standing over top of them, pointing a big finger, saying those words:

you are bad. you are a mistake. you are broken. you are defective. you are a disappointment. you are wrong.

you might jot down whatever you see, hear, or notice that aggressive person saying to your hurt inner child. it will be harsh, it will hurt your heart, but that's all part of bringing this shame out of the darkness and into the light.

you might also notice that this imposing, harsh figure sounds an awful lot like someone from your life. often, with shame, someone in our life will show up and be a mirror for the shame we feel inside – they reflect back to us what we are already feeling inside, what we are already saying to ourselves. and when they do, we take that as confirmation, as evidence, that the voice of shame was correct all along. we *believe* that we are bad, and someone comes along and *says* that we are bad, and so we believe it to be true even more *deeply* to our core. shame festers.

now here is the most important part of this exercise: grab some paper and pens... your job now is to **write a love letter** to your ashamed inner child.

the antidote for festering shame is **a shower of compassion** so that's what you need to do in your letter. let the compassion flow... your inner child is in desperate need of some love if that aggressive stuff is what they have been hearing for a long time!

what do they need to hear? what truth do they need to know? what do they need to remember moving forward? what love, compassion, empathy, can you shower them with now? let it all flow.

for bonus points, there is one more thing you can do to heal that shame, and that is to **share it with someone else**.

we know that shame festers in the darkness. bringing it into the light by writing a love letter is a great first step. but it is a bit like those comfort zones we talked about earlier: if you keep the shame inside your head, or inside your notebook, it is still hiding.

plus, next to compassion, the best antidote for shame is **empathy**.

empathy is when someone says: *me too*.

empathy is someone getting down into the darkness with you and shining that light of awareness on shame, together. there is immense power in empathy — in sharing your darkness with someone else. that's why shame doesn't want you to do it!

just as someone in your life can be a mirror for your shame, someone can also be a mirror for your compassion, if only you let them in.

when you share your shame with someone else, and when they say: you are not alone, me too! that belief of 'i am bad' begins to shift into: hmmmm.... maybe i am not alone in this. maybe i am not broken after all. maybe it's not just me. maybe i am actually normal!

moving forward from this exercise, please try to remember your inner child. when you notice that you are beating yourself up — when you notice that voice of shame pipe up — ask yourself: *would i talk to a child like that? would i talk to my best friend like that?*

of course not! so why would you talk to yourself like that? it's time to switch the station: instead of beating yourself up, love yourself up! be compassionate with yourself and change your language from 'i am a mistake' to 'i made a mistake' because shame is the biggest barrier to your healing. it's time to let it go.

we RISE when we heal.

fear.

fear is one of the most powerful forces that can keep you stuck. in fact this is the job of fear: to warn you and protect you from danger – to protect you from the bad things out there – to keep you safe, small, and same... especially as you take steps to RISE up and shine.

remember that inner dragon? he is on high alert thanks to fear. much of what we feel stuck with will have fear at the core... as you spiral with your stuff, somewhere under those layers you will often find fear.

just like we are *ashamed of our shame* and so we keep it hidden inside, we are also *afraid of our fear*. it's a self-perpetuating cycle of feeling it and avoiding it and giving in to it that keeps us spinning.

what is the way out?

stand inside the fire.

as garth brooks[10] beautifully sings: life is not tried it is merely survived if you're standing outside the fire.

we need to be able to face the fire – face our fear – head on, and jump in. this strategy is about bringing our fears into the light so that they no longer fester in the darkness.

name your fear.

we name it to tame it. and while there is a long list of things we could be afraid of in life, the truth is that we often don't see our fear very clearly (because it is so hard to look at it straight on) — we think we are afraid of whatever is on the surface but when we peel away layers we get closer to the truth.

for instance, we might think we are afraid of failure, but when we dig deeper we could find that we are actually afraid of success. so really go exploring and face your fear head on. consider everything you are afraid doing, being, feeling, facing, exposing, happening...

here are some common fears to get you started:

failure
success
change
nothing changing
mediocrity
outshining others
uncertainty
rejection
loneliness
getting it wrong
getting attacked
losing love
losing money
losing status

losing control
losing freedom
missing out
messing up
being too late
being too much
being not enough
being judged
being hurt
the unknown

once you have named your fear, check in with it...

explore the fear.

ask: is this real? is this true? is this helpful to you in some way? or is it holding you back?

does the fear point to *real* danger or *perceived* danger? fear knows no difference, our dragon brain reacts the same way. so we need to get good at knowing the difference ourselves — try to tune into your intuition, tap into the wisdom of your body, listen to the voice of real you.

ask: *where does the fear come from?* sometimes we take on fear that isn't even our own or that is no longer helpful to us.

once you've explored your fear a bit, the next step is to...

let the fear play out.

that thing that you are most afraid of? imagine it actually happening... your worst fear comes true. imagine it.

ask: *and then what will happen? and then what? and what else?*

let it all play out, let it all unfold, let all that fear actually happen in your mind's eye (or onto your page if you are brainstorming).

when we let it play out – when we imagine our worst fear and all of the consequences – it actually helps us to understand if it is even likely! if it is true, real, or helpful. if it really is as horrible as it seems in the darkness. maybe in the light of day, this fear is actually not so bad!

plus our brains begin to start finding answers, solutions, responses... plans B and C. this helps us to know that we can actually navigate even the worst thing happening. and if ever our fears do come true, they are often quite manageable because our brain already found the answer. in our minds, we've already dealt with it!

lastly, letting the fear play out helps with discernment. when you have all of those possibilities in front of you, you just might decide that you can be afraid *and also* take action anyways.

you can be courageous.

courage is not about being *not afraid*... it's about *being afraid AND being brave* enough to take action at the same time. being brave is about being true to your true self, trusting your inner real voice, following the path of what you know to be right... for you.

we have two choices when it comes to fear:

we can be afraid, and also be brave, and go ahead and do the thing we know in our core that we need to do, and become less afraid as we go, and keep doing.

or we can be afraid, and do nothing, and still be afraid, and prove your fear to be right and cement it in even further, and still do nothing.

which one keeps you stuck and which one helps you to move forward? i think you know!

being brave is not something you are born with, it's something you learn, practice, and keep building in yourself. you won't always FEEL brave, and you will often still feel afraid, but you can also BE brave.

you can choose to stand inside the fire.

do you remember the times in your life you did feel brave?

why did you feel brave in that situation? what happened next? could you replicate that situation to help you feel more brave now? or could you find what is missing from this situation now?

make a list of what will happen if you are brave and what will happen if you aren't. compare the pain of taking the chance to the pain of staying where you are and missing out.

just think: **if not now, then when? if not this, then what?**

it might also help if you don't do it for *you*. tap into your inner, brave superhero... show up and do it for the cause, do it for the people that need you, do it because the world needs it. **if not you, then who?** when you think of it this way, your fear is selfish... when you don't be brave you are robbing the world of whatever it is you long to do.

so build up some fight in you... get angry, get passionate, get fired up. tap into your inner rebel with a *'just watch me!'* attitude... anything that helps you ignite that fire of courage inside of you.

you might be afraid of where you are going, who you are being, and how you will do it all... but you can still be fuelled by WHY you are doing it.

you can let your why be what drives you forward. and you can add even more fuel to your tank when you celebrate your bravery. collect evidence of your bravery! anchor into the feeling of what brave feels like in your life.

you've got this.

25 years ago when i moved away to university, my mom gave me a framed print from mary ann radmacher[11] and it still hangs right beside me in my office. it's a reminder of the person she saw in me, the person i want to be: *the jump is so frightening between where i am and where i want to be. but for all i may become, i will close my eyes and leap.*

we RISE when we are brave.

lack.

lack of time. lack of energy. lack of focus. lack of capacity.

these are actually all related... they are all types of *currency* in your life. you only have so much time, so much energy, so much you can focus on, so much you can manage at once, so you need to choose where you spend your currency.

and these things are all types of *excuses* too... in fact they are often our first, easiest excuse because it is just so damned logical! when you want to *avoid* doing something your brain gives you some very handy, logical reasons, such as: *i have no time, it's not the right time, i need more time...*

when your time is busy... your energy is spent and you just don't have the capacity to focus on even one more thing! it becomes easier and easier to avoid as well as easier to focus on the lack in your life.

it's time to take back control of your time... and your energy and your focus... you need to be a...

savvy spender.

if your time, your energy, your focus, your attention, your capacity is your *currency* then you get to decide how and where you *spend it*. you decide where it goes.

because: **where you spend it, or where you send it, that's what will grow.**

think about that for a moment.

- → what is something in your life that feels like a drain on your energy?
- → where is there something that takes a lot of your time?
- → what is taking up your focus and attention right now?

now imagine that thing just growing in power... expanding and stretching. it's not going away, in fact it will continue to require more and more of your time, energy, and focus.

is that what you want? do you actually want that thing to grow?

what we focus on expands. what we carry around grows heavier. what we insist on, we invest in. this includes where we spend our time and energy. so we have got to choose wisely!

everything you say yes to, everything you add to your calendar or to do list, everything you carry in your mental load and emotional load... you invest in *all* of that.

so take responsibility for your time, energy, and focus. we all get the same number of minutes in a day, we all have a finite amount of energy... we just each choose to spend it differently!

how do we become a savvier spender?

here are some ideas to help you. ask...

→ **would you put it on a billboard?**

in other words, is this thing that you are investing in that important to you? is it what you want to be known for? is it what you really want to grow in strength and power and size?

→ **is this the best use of you?**

only do what only *you* can do! do the stuff that really lights you up or taps into your unique strengths and talents. otherwise, let someone else take care of it for you.

→ **is this your zone of genius?**

it's amazing how much time we spend in our zones of incompetence or competence – the yuck stuff and the meh stuff. let someone else say yes to that stuff and be in *their* zone of genius! this is one of my favourite ways to say no to something that i am asked to do or be part of: *sorry, it's not my zone of genius. i hope you find the right person.*

→ **what else could you be doing?**

every *yes* is a *no* to something else. for every place you spend your energy, focus, or time there is another place that is neglected. we often spend more time on things than we need to or we spend time on stuff that isn't really all that important to us. get in the habit of asking yourself: *is this actually where i want to spend? what else could i be doing?*

→ **what will you give up in order to do the thing you say you want to do?**

this is a big one. we say we want to do certain things in our life: create, learn, explore, improve, play, practice... but then we use time or energy or focus as the excuse for not being able doing those things! we only have so much time and energy to spend, so we need to decide what the priority is.

don't give up what matters to you or what is important in your life (like sleep!!)... that will just drain your bucket even further... but give up the stuff that is wasting your time or keeping you safe, small, same, or stuck (like binge watching tv or mindlessly scrolling social media perhaps!)

→ **what is your time language like?**

let's think about money currency for a moment. when it comes to money mindset you might hear people say positive money mantras like: *i love money and money loves me! there is plenty to go around. i have everything i need.* well time is a currency too and what do you often hear people say about it: *there is not enough time! time goes too fast! where did the time go?*

we can be savvy spenders by being savvier with how we treat time in our words, and our beliefs: *time is on my side. i have all the time in the world. there is time for everything that matters. this is how i choose to spend my time.*

→ **where is the blame?**

sometimes we really *don't* have the time, the energy, or the capacity – life might indeed be too busy, we might have other priorities, we might in fact need more time to do something because of certain circumstances. and that's ok! but are you *blaming* time? *(ugh! there is never enough time!)* or perhaps you are beating yourself up? *(i stuck, i should have done this by now!)*

let's stop the blame, stop letting time and timelines rule us. just **own your choice.** instead of saying: *i really want to write a book but i have no time. i should have started by now but my job and my kids take up all my time!* try saying instead: *i really want to write a book. and the time for that is next winter when our life is a little less hectic.*

remember your bucket: there are some things in your life that are bucket fillers and others that are bucket drainers. your time, energy, and focus can act as both — you can spend your currency on stuff that fills your bucket or you can spend it and completely drain your bucket. you can end up filling up your bucket with a whole lot of stuff that you don't really want to carry around with you — stuff that takes space away from the stuff you really do want in your life.

so be a savvy spender. and be protective of your bucket! make good choices.

no mojo.

no drive. no motivation. no gumption. no get up and go.

you are stuck and you kind of don't even care that you are stuck. because you just don't have the energy to get unstuck.

instead of focusing on the right here and now – focusing on the stuckness you feel right now and focusing on your lack of mojo – let's look ahead at your destination... on where you are going and why.

what is it that you have no mojo for? you can't get to your destination without any fuel in your tank. so check in with whatever it is you feel like you have no mojo for anymore, or ever, and work backwards.

remember your destination dream? picture it in your mind's eye. ask:

→ do i really want that?
→ does that feel like me?
→ why is this something i need to do?

picture the journey to get there in your mind's eye. ask:

→ how i am planning to get there?
→ can i do it my way?
→ can i get excited about the steps i need to take?
→ does this really get me where i want to be?

picture your stuckness right now, your feeling of no mojo. ask:

→ what am i avoiding / procrastinating on?
→ why is my fuel tank empty?

work backwards from where you want to be all the way back to where you are right now, and look for resistance.

is it a matter of fear, doubt, worry, or lack? give yourself permission to shift these things – you have strategies in your toolbelt now!

or is it a matter that this thing you say you want to do but that you have no mojo for isn't really aligned with you anymore?

notice every time you say 'should': *that's what i should do. someone told me i should. i should because it's what i always do. i said i would so i should. it is what makes sense on paper so i should.*

you need to stop should-ing all over yourself.

give yourself permission to make a change here. tap into your inner badass rule breaker... your inner rogue, inner rebel, or inner maverick.

depending on your personality, this might feel kind of easy or kind of hard. some of us are natural rule breakers! but i believe there is a little bit of rebel in each of us.

maybe you met them when you were spending time with your inner child, your inner shadow hunter, or future you. maybe you can already sense them when you think of one of those words: rule-breaker, rogue, rebel, or maverick. maybe a picture pops into your head: teenage you, or cocky 20 year old you, or free spirit child-like you, or a you from one other situation in your life... one time where you broke the rules and it felt *oh so good*.

rebel you is there inside of you somewhere and now is when you need that energy! do a...

rebel yell.

and bring that rule-breaking energy forth! with a rebel yell you can give yourself permission to do it your way, to go your own way, to be absolutely unapologetically you.

here are some ideas for a 'rebel yell' that you can state out loud...

→ **who says?**

this is such a good question to ask. who says? who says i have to do it that way? who says that's the way it's always been done? who wrote that rule?

most of the time the rules we constrain ourselves with are completely arbitrary anyways — they are based on old stories and upper limits and comparison. those rules don't serve you. so break them!

be a rebel, shout it out: *who says?* break the rules. write your own rules.

→ **just watch me!**

this is some great rebel energy... the desire for showing people what you've got, what you're made of! when you realize that there is something that has been getting in the way of you doing what you say you want to do – face it, recognize it, and then go and do it anyways with some *'just watch me!' 'i will show you!' 'you aren't the boss of me!'* energy.

when you tell a rebel they *can't*, their immediate reaction is: *who says!* and *just watch me*. we really don't like being told what we *should do*.

→ **this is me.**

you've got to own who you are, embrace all of you (shadows and all!) and you've got to speak up and say it out loud: *hey world, this is me. you don't like it? too bad! it's not your thing? that's ok with me.*

→ **i've gotta be me.**

alignment is everything. if you don't feel like you can be you, if you aren't doing it your way, if it isn't a good match for who you are and how you work and what you really want... well it just isn't sustainable!

you will never keep your mojo for something that doesn't align... the 'shoulds' become a bucket drainer instead of a bucket filler, and you run out of fuel in your tank.

can you tweak your plans so they feel more like you? can you break out of the box that constrains you and go your own way? get creative, define it a new way, have some fun with it? it's your life, you only get one chance... so you've got to go your own way.

→ **i am done.**

sometimes we need to just give ourselves permission to be done. to say no, to stop what we are doing, to change the plan, to get rid of the stuff that is no longer serving you. all those 'shoulds' need to be decluttered right out of your lighthouse.

what are you done with? make a list. then give yourself permission to say that out loud to who needs to hear it. and then make a change. what do you do instead? whatever is simplest and funnest to you. that's the key.

let go of all of the shoulds: whatever everyone else is doing and whatever it is that you think you should be doing and whatever seemed like a good idea on paper. most of that is more complicated than it needs to be, and most if it doesn't align with who you are or where you are actually going anyways.

instead, ask yourself – if there were no rules, no shoulds, what would be:

- the simplest and funnest thing to do?
- the simplest and funnest way to make this happen?
- the simplest and funnest single step to take?

this is your permission to do *that*.

we RISE when we do it our way.

***

play more: this strategy is full of song titles! music is an awesome way to tap into that rebel energy – try making your own collection of songs that fires you up, that reminds you that you are the boss of you, that helps you tap into your inner badass rule breaker. find these songs on the lighthouse revolution playlist at karengunton.com/free

lost.

the feeling of being lost is so common. and it can show up in some different ways.

you feel like you've lost your sense of direction, you feel like you've lost your sense of purpose, you feel like you've lost yourself, or you feel like you've lost your drive. you don't know where you are going, who you are being, or why.

i know this feeling well. i felt like when i lost my mom i lost my self. i lost my knowing of who i was being, and where i was going, and why. people say to me: *you haven't lost yourself, you're still you! you just need time to heal, etc. etc.* but the truth is, it doesn't feel that way. the way it feels to me is *i am lost.* but i know i will find myself again... likely a new sense of self, of who i am now and what i will do with my next chapter.

this is what i believe to be true: each of us is here for a reason, there is something we are meant to do, someone we are meant to be, a light we are meant to shine.

your purpose, your calling, your mission, your legacy – whatever you want to call it – it is what you are meant to do. it is who you are meant to be.

do you remember who you were born to be, what you were born to do?

purpose is not actually a 'figure it out once' sort of thing... it is in fact the journey itself. by exploring who you are in the world you actually get closer to who you are meant to be.

i think of the journey as a spiral, with lots of layers. you might even think of it as an onion! we are always evolving, we are always growing and changing. so where you are at right now might be your purpose for right now. and then when you begin to feel like you are meant to be doing something more, or like the path you are on isn't where you want to go, or like you are being called to some new things, or like you have lost yourself... then it is time to peel away another layer and see where the journey takes you next.

seeking your purpose *is* your purpose. so is being authentically you, doing what lights you up, and doing what gives your life meaning.

there is a reason that your life's purpose or your soul's purpose is also often described as your calling.

you 'hear the call' or you 'feel called' to do something more, something different, something bigger or deeper or even scarier.

that is a sign to take another step on your purpose journey... to explore and see what unfolds next.

just think about your road so far... there was a time where you didn't feel lost. right? you felt a sense of purpose, you knew where you were going, what you were doing, who you were being, and why... something in your life gave you that sense of direction.

you are in a new place now, so you need to peel away some layers of that purpose and see what is next for you.

you need to...

choose your mission.

i like to use the word *mission* to describe having a sense of direction or purpose. it brings to mind the idea of creating a mission statement for your life or stating *'i am on a mission'* with your efforts and activities.

i believe that having a mission helps to give you a sense of self-fulfilment and adds more meaning to your everyday life.

the beauty is that your mission can be anything you want it to be. you choose it, define it, and declare it... for you!

you don't have to call it a mission, you can call it anything you like: quest, adventure, movement, awakening, transformation, disruption, revolution, invention, trail-blazing, embracing, exploring... whatever words help you get up in the morning with some direction, mojo, and purpose and do whatever you choose to do, shine your light in any way you choose.

it can be as simple as choosing one defining theme, value, character trait, or act: such as kindness, authenticity, gratitude, giving-back, or confidence.

or you can create a more complex mission such as a set of actions, behaviours, or rules to live by.

you could declare the kind of change you wish to see in the world (even if it is simply the world for your family, workplace, or community.)

or you could determine now what you want to be your legacy.

your mission can be about one or a combination of:

- who you are (your strengths and superpowers)
- what you are here to do (your purpose or calling)
- where you are going (your towards vision, the dream you have for yourself/others)
- how you want to live your life (your values, ideals, focus)
- your why (whatever drives you)

to create your very own mission statement for your life you can put all of these pieces together.

try it...

my name is:

i am: (*who* you are)

i am here to: (*what* you are here to do)

because: (*why* you do it)

i have this BIG dream: (*where* you are going)

so i am on a mission: (define it or declare it!)

your mission can act like an umbrella or a unifying theme that encompasses all of the different parts of your life: your interests, your work, your home, your relationships, your activities, and your sense of self.

a mission can help be a guiding direction for your life, so that you no longer feel so lost.

your mission is your 'fight song': *this is my fight song, take back my life song, prove i'm alright song... my power's turned on and i've still got a lot of fight left in me!* - Rachel Platten[12]

it's the soapbox you get up on, it's the line you draw in the sand, it's the change you want to see in the world... even just the world for one other person, even if that person is you.

your mission doesn't have to be big, it just needs to light you up inside, so that you can take back your mojo, fuel up your tanks, and shine.

we RISE when we have a reason.

yah, but...

even when you have strategies for the fear, the doubt, the worry, the overwhelms, the self-sabotage, the uncertainty – even if you do feel stronger in all of these areas – you may still catch the voice in your head saying something like this:

yah, but...

- yah, but what if i do fail?
- yah, but what if i end up screwing this all up?
- yah, but what if it never really happens?
- yah, but what if i actually am not good enough to do this?

it's like even with all the tools you use to get unstuck and RISE above anything that has been standing in your way... that voice just has to get in one last whisper, just to keep you small and safe and stuck.

yah, but...

we need to give this whisper a new job... the job of saying:

yah, but what if it all works out?!

to do that we need to give that whisper a good, positive outlook to focus on (instead of all the worry, doubt, fear, lack). we are going to pick...

the ONE possibility.

that one that you actually want to focus on.

every time you say a *yah but...* you've thought of something that might indeed happen. you've brought that possibility into existence with your thoughts. and yah, it actually might happen that way. sure.

but there are also a thousand things that might happen, a million possibilities that can occur.

so let's name them all!

make a list: this might happen, this might happen, this might happen. let yourself name all of the possibilities from horrible to not so bad to ok to good to great to freaking awesome! name as many of the infinite possibilities and combinations of possibilities as you can... try for 100 possibilities! get them all out on the page.

now circle ONE.

the one that actually makes you feel hopeful, excited, motivated. the one that you actually want to focus on bringing into existence.

mary morrisey[13], in her tedx talk *the hidden code for transforming dreams into reality*, says: *everything is created twice. first it has to be a thought before it can become a thing.*

so let yourself choose the ONE possible outcome, the one result, that you actually want to turn into a thing... and focus on that one.

the one possibility.

it is not helpful to you RISING to focus on the worst of all the possible outcomes... to let this whisper of 'yah but...' keep you small, safe, same, and stuck.

remember the work you have already done to move past the fear, the worry, the doubt, or the uncertainty...

say out loud: hey, wait just a second! i left that worry back in that old box of stuckness that used to keep me from rising.

and then reply back to that whisper...

yah, but remember, **this is the one possibility i hold to be true.** this is the one i will focus on.

grief.

the first version of this book did not have a chapter on grief.

of course i had experienced grief myself and i had witnessed many people in my life go through grief. i assumed it was something everyone experienced at some point or another and you just sort of dealt with it, i guess? it didn't occur to me that grief might be something that you truly became stuck in — stuck and lost, unable to move forward — until i experienced that myself.

so here we are... a chapter on grief.

the tricky thing is that the only strategy that i have found, in all of my research and all of my talking to people about grief, is that to deal with grief you must grieve.

not a very fancy strategy is it? *oh you're sad? well then you need to feel sad.*

but it is what works. if you don't allow yourself to grieve — if you avoid it, if you tell yourself you should feel better by now, if you tell yourself that other people have it worse, if you tell yourself that you shouldn't even feel sad about this thing — that ends up being what gets you stuck.

feeling is healing.

this is true of any of the things we've talked about in this book, of course: awareness, acceptance, exploring, understanding, honouring, feeling.

in order to heal, we must allow ourselves to feel.

so i apologize for not having a more snazzy strategy... i haven't even got a catchy tune you can sing when you want to remember what to do. all i can say is the only way to get to the other side of grief is to go right through the middle of it. our feelings, including grief, aren't just little bumps that we can avoid in our path, they are tunnels... and the only way through is through.

so please let yourself be sad, mad, disappointed, dejected, lost, adrift, unanchored. feel it. talk about it. write about it. make heartbreak playlists like you did when you were 13. cry in your bed and snuggle your dog. not gonna lie, letting yourself feel all the feelings hurts, so much so that many of us avoid it, but after that comes healing.

there is one thing that i think we need to be better aware of: you can feel grief – deep, painful, heart-aching grief – not just from losing people but also from losing things: money, a trip, a job, activities that bring you joy, aspects of life that fill your bucket, progress towards something, a way of life, future plans, dreams you hold for yourself.

grief happens when we are torn from something we love, value, or cherish. you can only grieve something that truly mattered to you... **it is an acknowledgement from your soul.** and when you think about it that way it is really important to honour that.

one way that you can find yourself stuck in grief is by not honouring that you are indeed grieving something you've lost.

you may have made a careful, conscious choice or decision to let go of something, and still feel grief. you may think you ought to be grateful for what you *do* have, and still feel grief. other people may have lost something that seems far greater or more profound, and you can still feel grief.

your grief is real.

please don't discount it. don't shame yourself into trying not to feel it. don't assume that it doesn't really matter. don't tell yourself to feel something else instead — in fact it is possible to feel grief *and also* feel grateful.

i heard something in conversation one day that i thought was so good. one person got choked up with tears and grief while talking and began to explain why. the other person interrupted and said: *it's ok. we don't explain ourselves when we begin laughing in a conversation. a person's joy is obvious. it is the same for grief — no need to explain why we begin to* cry. i can see that you are grieving and i can see the deep love you have for what you lost. i honour that.

so just like you do not have to justify your happiness please don't feel like you must justify your grief.

i find that it helps to have a picture in my mind about how grief works. it's not a linear journey from one spot to another, something you travers to get to a destination where the grief is gone. instead, i think grief is more like waves crashing into you on whatever path you were already on. there you were, going along in life, and then bang. a massive wave knocks you where you stand.

consider that waves have both size and frequency. when you first experience grief the waves are huge, crashing, monstrous things that can knock your breath away. and they are relentless – coming at you one right after the other – so relentless that we might decide it is better to avoid them all together.

but over time, if you allow yourself to feel, the waves get a little smaller, they come less frequently, you get better at navigating them. you might predict when one is coming, or a big one may hit you out of the blue, but you know that it's just a wave, you can ride it out and you'll come through the other side.

the waves never go away, they will forever be with you on your journey because the loss is now a part of you, but you begin to live with it... a new normal.

when they come, take a breath, allow the waves of grief to wash over you.

one little strategy that has helped me to grieve is to **make note of what is beautiful** in my time of loss. i look for the beauty in dying and in death, i look for the beauty amongst our pain and heartbreak, i look for the beauty in the smallest quietest moments. even the beautiful things hurt – in fact they hurt so much that sometimes i want to look away instead of taking note and taking it in – but the hurt has so much love in it and maybe that is what helps.

if you are finding that you are stuck in grief, not able yet to move forward, try looking back at the loss that you are still grieving and look for the beauty. it will still hurt, but remember that is the point... it is a gateway into feeling the feelings. feel so you can heal.

one last thing may help, when you are ready. you may be aware of experiencing different phases in your grief or loss – denial, anger, depression, acceptance – but i would urge you to remember these don't happen on any timeline or even in any logical order. naming them is simply about allowing yourself to feel them. however you experience these things is true for you! everyone grieves differently, so please don't put yourself on some sort of timeline or compare yourself to others.

there seems to be an unspoken shame associated with grief: how we do it, the timeline, the way it changes us. be kind to yourself through your grief.

plus there is another phase of grief that you may wish to explore: **finding meaning.**

finding meaning is not a way to bypass the pain of feeling your grief, rather it is a way to navigate who you are on the other side. grief changes you. if you let it, the pain, anger, denial, and depression of grief can close you off from the world. finding meaning is a way to open ourselves up again. this is not about finding meaning in death or loss, rather it is about finding meaning in YOU... in what you do next. ask: *what can i do now that is meaningful?*

the more real and honest and open you are about how you feel – the more you let yourself feel your feelings – the less stuck in the pit of grief you will become. your talking about, experiencing, or living with grief doesn't mean you are *stuck* in grief... stuck is when you cannot step forward or do the things that give your life meaning. stuck is not being able to find the new you on the other side.

grief does change you.

when you lose something or someone you lose a part of YOU too. you must grieve that lost part of yourself: *i miss the me that she knew. i miss who i* was when i had that in my life. i miss that version of my story.

let yourself be changed. not to close yourself off but to open yourself up. when you feel the depth of your feelings, when you find beauty and meaning, you get braver.

feel your grief and let it change you.

***

play more: for resources, books, and more about the stages of grief, including david kessler's book <u>finding meaning</u> visit grief.com

inertia.

inertia: a disinclination to move; lifelessness, inertness, inactivity; you're stuck. you aren't taking action.

why?

procrastination, perfection, paralysis. the voice of fear. the voice of doubt, uncertainty, or unworthiness. self-sabotage. overwhelm. hiding.

these are all things that can get in the way of taking action, and we've talked about strategies for each of them.

but then what? you do the inner work, you work on your stuff... and then you've got to take forward action! action is the opposite of inertia, the opposite of stuckness.

sometimes you have to take action even while you are also working on your stuff. sometimes you've gotta...

JFDI. just fucking do it.

truthfully, there will always be reasons to stay where you are: to stay small, safe, same, secure, stuck. even as you clear the stuff that is getting in your way, new stuff will simply come up to take its place.

JFDI is a phrase i love, it reminds me to just get out of my own way and just take even one step... to feel the fear (or doubt or worry) and *just do it anyways.*

what will help you to JFDI?

here are some ideas to try:

→ **it's not a tattoo.**

you don't have to have it all figured out. it doesn't have to be perfect. it's not a tattoo — you can actually change it as you go, you can learn as you go, you can make it better, you can stop, you can try something new.

→ **take imperfect action on purpose.**

when we wait for perfection we will probably never even get there. plus we are so attached to that perfection we aren't even willing to learn or change as we go. do it imperfectly on purpose so that you can actually be open to improving.

→ **done is better than perfect.**

that picture of perfection that you have in your mind... that picture of what you want to happen, of what it will be like, how it will all look... you are the only one who can see that! no one else can see that picture of perfection that you hold. to them, from their perspective, whatever you do is exactly what you meant for. in other words, no one is judging you on your perfection but you.

→ **start today.**

the time will never be right. you will never really be ready (or enough or perfect.) but one month or one year from now you will wish you started today! we all need to start somewhere, we all start at zero. and when you take one step the next steps will appear.

→ **start where you can.**

take the easiest step first. you can build your confidence and belief and courage as you go. start in the middle if you have to, work out the rest later. fake it till you make it if it helps... act as if. start where you feel comfortable and expand from there.

→ **start where you are.**

you don't have to be the expert, you don't have to know it all, you don't have to have it all figured out, you don't need to wait until you are more than you are right now. you can start exactly where you are... do what you can, say what you can, offer what you can.

→ **start right now.**

mel robbins[14] wrote a great book called <u>5 second rule</u> as a strategy to help people take action. the premise is simple: as soon as the thought to do something happens, count down 5, 4, 3, 2, 1 and do it. just like a rocket ship taking off, just do it. the countdown helps us to take action before that inner dragon can pipe up and stop us in our tracks.

→ **WWLD? what would 'lighthouse me' do?**

remember lighthouse you? real you, wise you, future you... the you who is confident, courageous, and worthy? just ask yourself: *what would lighthouse me do?* or: *what would lighthouse me tell me do?* and then go do that.

→ **embrace the FFT.**

brené brown[15], in her podcast *unlocking us*, talks about the FFT: the fucking first time. as she fabulously says: *this shit is hard y'all.* so recognise and accept it for what it is, a fucking first time that is going to be messy and hard. be kind to you and keep going!

i encourage you to have action taking as your final step no matter how you decide to get unstuck. do the awareness work, do the shifting work and then take some sort of courageous, inspired action. (we'll talk more about your next steps in the conclusion of this book.)

go with your instinct, go with what calls to you, go with the thing that scares you... count down 5,4,3,2,1 and then do something towards where you want to be (away from where you've been stuck.)

we will often say to ourselves things like: *i wish i had more confidence. if only i wasn't afraid. i just need some more mojo, more time, more readiness. i want this, but...* we make excuses. we avoid. we procrastinate.

we need to change our language, and we need to change our actions.

we need to replace 'i want this to work out' with 'i choose for this to work out.' and then ask ourselves: 'now what am i prepared to do about it?'

and then JFDI.

we RISE when we take action.

conclusion: stepping forward

rise. 330

now what?

you now have a number of strategies in your toolbelt that will help you get unstuck and RISE – strategies for awareness, strategies for shifting and healing your stuff, and specific strategies for various kinds of stuckness you might be experiencing.

you won't remember all of these.

but i hope you will remember that they are here... i hope that you will come back to these ideas and keep choosing new ones to try out and play with.

choose your adventure.

i said from the beginning that this book is designed to be a 'choose your own adventure' – you pick and choose the strategies that you need in order to RISE right now.

you can layer them together – choose an awareness strategy, a shifting strategy, and a specific unstucking strategy – to create your own practice... something practical, doable, and that makes a real difference to you.

here are some ideas for implementing the strategies in this book... for taking the ideas shared here and actually doing the work.

→ choose one thing you want to work on and choose one way to work on it, focus on that one strategy

→ choose one thing you want to work on and throw everything you can at it, try out multiple strategies and see what helps

→ create one new daily practice which can be a combination of a couple of things, your own unique strategy

make it a thing.

whatever you decide to try, whatever you are going to use to work on changing your stuckness, actually make it *a thing you do*. do not let it remain something that you plan to do or want to do but never get around to.

we RISE when we decide to rise.

name it.

call it a challenge, project, experiment, practice, exercise, operation, activity, endeavour, program, experience, quest, adventure, exploration, game plan, journey, or something else.

use words that work for you.

i used to use the word challenge a lot – i would set myself a '30 day worthiness challenge' or whatever. but that word doesn't really work for me right now – challenges feel, well, too challenging! now i would probably call it a '30 day journey' but some people find the word journey annoying.

so pick something you are proud to say out loud and you are excited to move ahead with.

make it fun! let it be funny or silly or sweet or weird... remember that play and fun is a powerful tool to change your energy around the inner work you do.

share it.

i know that can be the scary bit, but remember what we've learned about stretching your comfort zone... and remember what we've learned about how things fester in the darkness. not only does sharing your 'thing' open you up to more empathy, awareness, and understanding but it helps to keep you accountable. you will actually practice your strategy if you announce that you are!

if it feels weird to share what you are working on you can blame it on me. say something like: *my teacher has given me this weird homework, i have to do a 30 day challenge to ____ and i will be sharing my progress.*

how can you share it? social media is perfect for this sort of thing... you don't have to share everything you are working on and noticing and spiralling with, but you can share something to keep you accountable and to keep you noticing! try making a #hashtag for your challenge and sharing a little something each day... you could simply write a little blurb, or take a photo, or take a selfie! you could do a live video or a daily story.

you might even create a little accountability group with a few other people who also want to work on the same thing that you do: confidence, or worthiness, or fear, or overwhelm, or whatever you are focusing on! you could create a group on social media, or a private chat thread, or even meet up in real life!

if you don't want to share your challenge quite so publicly on social media or with friends, at least have a way to do the challenge at home and make it a 'thing'- let your partner or your kids know what you are working on, post up a calendar or use a white board to keep track.

do it for 30 days.

why 30? in my experience, 30 days gives you enough time to go through all sorts of stages of discomfort, comfort, difficulty, exploration, stretching, and noticing. it also gives you enough time to really make these strategies a new habit, to truly shift things within yourself, and to start doing things a new way... you actually do notice results!

also, in my experience, it is hard to go beyond 30 days. you might try a 40 day challenge, a 55 day challenge, a 100 day challenge... whatever floats your boat! but many people will get bored or get off track if you make your challenge too long. and most don't really get the full impact if your challenge is too short. some people go for 21 days but i think 30 days is enough time to stretch you, and your willingness to play and explore remains high.

plus – 30 days is perfect to try over the course of one month! easy! (or if the month has 31 days: do that!)

***

*play more: if you share your challenge include the hashtag **#iamariser**, i would love to follow along and cheer you on!*

track it.

tracking is one of the most powerful tools for implementation. **what you track, you transform.**

tracking is not about keeping track of what day you are on of your personal challenge, it is about **noticing** what is happening each day.

noticing how you feel. noticing your discomfort, your boredom, your avoidance or procrastination, your successes too.

remember that we began this journey to RISE with awareness, and that is how we will continue moving forward. it is in the noticing that we really begin to shift things.

choosing to track your journey is choosing self-responsibility for your own personal transformation. you are taking charge of your own RISING – you are saying this is what i am going to work on over the next however many days and i am serious about doing it so i will track how it goes each day.

how can you keep track of your progress?

again... choose something that works in your life but also feels FUN and energises you.

→ day planner
→ notebook
→ bullet journal
→ calendar

→ chalk board/whiteboard/window/mirror
→ a chart with gold stars or stamps or tick boxes
→ colouring in sheet (colour in one element per one day of progress)
→ online app

some people are motivated by rewards, others don't like to 'break the chain'. some people need to schedule in very specific activities, others need loads of flexibility. some people love creativity, colour, and artistic expression, others prefer quiet simplicity.

tracking is about knowing what works for you and using it to your advantage to create change, but it is also about noticing along the way and using what you notice to help you too!

as you are tracking through your progress there are some things to note:

→ **self-compassion**

remember tracking is not about having to do the thing every day – so it's not about shame or guilt or beating yourself up either – it's about noticing what happens along the journey. if you don't do the thing, if you forget, if you do it badly, if you get to busy… just notice. be kind to yourself! and then keep going.

→ **adjusting**

maybe you notice things that are working well, making a difference. maybe you notice things that are not. adjust your plans along the way! do what works, ditch what doesn't, try try again!

→ **stretching**

you might notice that things start to feel a bit easier... this can be a great opportunity to stretch your comfort zone or push yourself a little further. this is all about growth, learning, and moving forward. don't get complacent!

→ **celebration**

remember that celebrating your successes is an important strategy for self-leadership. when we track progress we give ourselves lots of opportunity to celebrate! you might even want to plan some great rewards for yourself in advance.

→ **confirmation**

remember the bingo game? tracking gives you a great opportunity to play bingo with yourself. predict what is going to be hard, uncomfortable, weird, helpful, fun, boring and then notice it along the way, and do pat yourself on the back for being so self-aware.

just remember — tracking is simply about noticing. **use what you notice to help you RISE.**

a story: #selfielove challenge.

my one big challenge is about enoughness and one of the strategies that i wanted to explore for myself is self-love as a path to self-worth. if we want others to believe that we are worthy, valuable, deserving, enough... we must first think these things of ourselves.

so in order to engage in an act of radical self-love, i set myself a challenge to post a selfie every day for an entire month... and, also as an act of self-love, to post the photo WITHOUT beating myself up... to love myself up instead.

at the time, i was never one for posting a lot of selfies on social media, so this whole #selfielove challenge was indeed a genuine challenge for me!

on day one i was a little bit uncomfortable: my 'go to' reaction upon taking my own photo was indeed to beat myself up: *look at those bags under your eyes, what is going on with your hair, wow that's a terrible angle.*

i caught myself and stopped myself... looked at myself in the eyes and said out loud to my image on my phone: *i love you. just as you are. you are enough. just as you are.* and then i posted the damn thing!

by day three i was getting the hang of it... posting my selfie and loving myself up in the process, feeling really good about it!

then on day four i woke up with three giant pimples growing on my face. i looked in the mirror and just started to laugh: *hello upper limit problem... nice to see you today!*

(remember that upper limit to how good we feel? when we activate our upper limit — when we step towards our true potential — our fear sets in and subconsciously we sabotage ourselves so that we stay in the same, safe, small, comfy space where nothing bad happens.)

in that moment i could see my three pimply pals for what they were... i had set off an upper limit of self-love and self-worth! i quickly posted my selfie anyways... continuing my big leap towards loving myself and feeling good about myself.

after that, the daily #selfielove continued on easily... i used it as a chance to explore and share the things that i do in my life that are indeed acts of self-love. once i realized how easy it was starting to feel to post a selfie each day i figured it was time to step it up.

in week three i set myself a challenge to state out loud in the comments what i love about myself... oh wow, that was hard! but it was good, as it pushed me to really love myself up in a bigger way!

and then in week four i decided that i would share some of the aspects of me that maybe not everyone knows about... embracing, owning, and loving those parts of me that i keep hidden away sometimes. sharing the authentic me, the real me, the imperfect me.

in the end, the 31 day #selfielove challenge ended up being a very powerful journey. i absolutely do feel that i built up my self-worth. but i actually experienced many lessons, beyond self-love. here's what i learned...

on consistency:

i learned that setting a daily challenge and tracking it in some way works really well for me (this is also how i wrote this book in just 24 days with NaNoWriMo) – so a daily photo posted to instagram was a great fit. i don't like to miss a day once i have the chain going, plus this was a way of pushing out of my comfort zone a little (versus something like just writing in my journal why i love myself!)

on ego:

a few people mentioned to me that they didn't think they could do a #selfielove challenge like this because they felt it would be egotistical or narcissistic to post a photo of themselves every day...

i mean who wants to see you talk about you all the time! anytime i teach about worthiness, confidence, self-value, or self-belief the 'ego fears' come into play somehow.

here's my take on it.

self-love, self-worth, self-esteem, self-confidence, self-value... these are indeed acts of the SELF... of the higher self, the inner self, the soul. the higher self is all about evolving, creating, growing. narcissism is an act of the ego which is all about the here and now, material existence and self-preservation.

so self-love and self-leadership actually has nothing to do with ego: especially when we share our self-leadership story from a place of humility *(i am not better than you, i am simply enough)*, empathy *(loving myself up so that i have lots of love to give others)*, integrity *(walking my own talk)*, and vulnerability *(sharing the real me, pimples and all)*.

on visibility:

many people also told me that a #selfielove challenge like this definitely provokes their fear of being visible and prominent... again that whole *"no one wants to see my face for 31 days!"* fear. i think this is even more of a reason to do a #selfielove challenge – we must push out of our comfort zone and remember that our light is not meant to be hidden away.

remember those comfort zones and those zones of visibility: we must keep pushing our own boundaries past what feels a little bit uncomfortable, keep expanding into new levels of voice, visibility, authenticity, vulnerability, and more. this is how we grow and step towards our highest, brightest potential!

on stepping up:

depending on your situation there are ways to step up your #selfielove challenge and make it even more powerful.

try not just posting a photo, but looking at yourself right in the eyes of the photo and naming the things that you love about yourself. then try listing them right in your comments, or adding text onto your image!

try sharing the real you... imperfect, authentic, quirky, weird, wonderful you! try no make-up or bad hair, pjs or worn out gym wear, bed time or morning chaos. remember this is about loving yourself as you are, because you are exactly *enough* just as you are.

try sharing (and loving) the things about you that you often keep hidden: your secret dreams, your obsessions, your shadow side, your spirituality or beliefs, your hidden talents or gifts, your greatest challenges... it is very hard to shine your light in the world when you are busy hiding you.

on your life:

our inner critic wants to point out the stuff we can't or shouldn't do. our ego reminds us of our past failures and our fears of the future. we mustn't let these moments become the album of our lives... we must fill the pages with snapshots of love, worthiness, celebration, value, gratitude, success, confidence... this is what we do when we post our #selfielove: we fill the pages with the stories of our highest, brightest self.

this way, when we flip through our life's album, the story of self-worth is the one we see most prominently (rather than the unworthy one).

when i mentioned doing the #selfielove challenge, one of my community members shared that she thought it was an important way to document your life. social media helps to create an album of your life and your work, and putting yourself into that album is so important.

ask yourself: *what do i want to be known for?* share more of that. share more of you.

unworthiness is about feeling not enough. not smart enough, not good enough, not 'big' enough, not special enough... whatever that voice is saying. the opposite of not enough is plenty. it's abundance. and not an abundance of what you have... but of who you are.

#selfielove is about recognizing and honouring the abundance of who you are. just as you are. because you are enough. you are worthy. you were born that way.

but wait.

what if you are feeling so stuck that it feels like no matter what you try, you just cannot move forward? when the whole 'make it a thing, do a 30 day challenge and track it' idea feels like an impossibility... when getting out of bed feels like an impossibility.

darkness is a black hole.

i noticed something during my time spent stuck and lost in the darkness... maybe you have noticed this at some point in your life too.

the very things that that will help us to find our way, move forward, or make a change become the very things we do not do for our self or give to our self.

self-love, self-care, self-compassion, self-motivation, self-guidance, self-healing... it is all easier to do when things are good. when we feel ignited, when we feel healthy and energetic and content, when things in life go according to 'plan'.

but when things are not good — when we experience a 'wreck', when things go off the rails, when we are lost in the darkness, when we are deeply stuck in our stuff — self-love and other acts of self-leadership are not so easy.

ironically those are the times when we need to love ourselves and lead ourselves even more!

when we feel ignited — lit up from within... focused, fired up, on purpose — it is easier to do the things that fill up our bucket, ignite out spark, and fuel our passion.

but when we are lost in the darkness, the very things that we know will help us to feel ignited again are the very things we resist, avoid, procrastinate, and hide from.

this is the cruel reality of the darkness: it creates its own self-fulfilling black hole.

your time in the darkness sucks away your desire to seek out the light and so the darkness grows even more powerful.

like the indigo girls[16] sing in <u>closer to fine</u>: *the darkness has a hunger that's insatiable, the lightness has a call that's hard to hear.*

and so what can we do?

i feel like we need to sort of sneak up, very slowly, very quietly, on those things that will ignite our spark again... take the smallest, babyest of steps.

it's a bit like making a fire. your light is just barely smouldering there under the coals — if you throw a big log onto it you are just going to smother the flame! so instead you add the tiniest bits of kindling... just the smallest of things... and wait for them to catch the flame. as the flame slowly, slowly builds up in strength, you can begin to add bigger pieces into the fire.

when you are burning bright – on fire, lit up from within – the big pieces are fun... you feel motivated and brave and empowered. (and some of you reading this might be very ready for the big pieces. that's great!)

but when it's just the tiniest of embers glowing in the darkness, everything big feels a little bit hard... you have to be gentle with your kindling.

take baby steps.

what is the smallest bit of kindling you can add to your flame right now? what is the tiniest step you can take to move yourself forward?

when i say baby steps i mean the babyest of steps possible... the most simple of things.

make a list of the things that fill your bucket, that are healing to you, that help you feel like real you or lighthouse you.

now for each of those things – what is the baby step version of that thing?

for example if one of your things is writing, could you maybe try texting a loved one a little story about your day?

- → if it's art, could you get a fun art app on your phone and start there?
- → if it's cooking up healthy, nourishing meals, could you start with drinking more water?
- → if it's walking on the beach could you just go park your car beside the beach and watch the waves for a while?
- → if it's running could you at least put on your shoes and remember how that feels?

perhaps these things seem silly – not even close to the actual changes you want to make in your life. but remember, the point is to start with the easiest thing you can actually manage, for today, and let it be a baby step towards where you really want to go.

here is a radical idea... **perhaps we can be stuck AND ALSO still move forward.**

if you were down in a dark hole, trying to find a way out, you would begin by moving, shifting little scoops of dirt out of your way. in doing so you are actually moving a little bit forward each time.

yes you are still stuck, it's still dark, but you aren't staying there in that hole. with your baby steps forward you are actually building your own tunnel out! eventually you won't feel quite so stuck... you will have more space, more air, more progress... you might even begin to see and feel the light shining through!

there is one last thing to watch out for when stuck in this dark hole.

remember back when we talked about awareness and the habits and behaviours that keep us in our stuck space... the sticky steps that may feel like you are 'doing something' but really you are just sliding back into the muddy hole.

now that you are aware of your sticky steps, as often as you can, make the choice to take a baby step instead.

we RISE even with baby steps.

a story: water & savasana.

when i was feeling lost in the darkness, i couldn't bring myself to do yoga. something i love, something that always fills my bucket became something too big, too hard. in an effort to perhaps add just a tiny bit of kindling to the embers of what was once my fire... i got up out of my bed and lay on the mat.

literally that is it. for as long as i could, as often as i could bring myself to do it, i just lay on the mat. this is an actual pose in yoga, called savasana, so i joked with my friends that it counted, right?

what i began to realise was how much it counted. it was a baby step. out of the darkness, out of my stuckness.

i couldn't make myself to go down to the beach for a walk. but i went outside and stood in the sunshine.

i didn't feel like spending time with anyone. but i typed out a couple of real, honest messages to best friends.

i noticed for me that one of the babyest of steps that made a difference was drinking water. it seems so silly to bother even sharing that as a 'strategy', but 'drinking more water' was a job i could manage – i couldn't write, i couldn't meditate, i couldn't create, i couldn't play, i couldn't share... but drinking water... i could leave my dark cave to do that.

slowly slowly the darkness receded.

slowly slowly the flame began to grow.

i also began to better notice my sticky steps... those daily actions and habits and behaviours that were keeping me stuck in the darkness.

a big one for me was mindlessly scrolling social media – not posting anything (there will be a huge gap in my 'facebook memories' because i didn't think i had anything worth posting) – just scrolling and feeling crappy.

another was not getting out of bed in the morning. i would send my kids off to school and climb right back into my bed and keep scrolling on my phone, reading fan fiction online, or watching netflix. (note: none of these things is inherently wrong! in fact i still love and do all of them. but for me, i noticed that starting the day with them was a sticky step keeping me in bed.)

i tried to be more aware of my sticky steps and noticing what was keeping me in my stuck place.

and i tried adding more baby steps into my life and my day.

savasana eventually did lead me back to yoga, which helped me get back to meditation, which helped me get back to journaling.

stepping outside onto the grass led me back to walking again. which got me listening to podcasts. which got inspiration flowing again.

reading through this book (because the thought of finishing it was just too hard to fathom so i simply just lay in bed in the dark and read what i had written so long ago) helped me to remember my why just a little, helped ignite my purpose again, just a little.

these little baby steps helped me to at least ask the question: *what baby step can i take next?*

and they helped because they were ridiculously simple and often quite broad. *move your body. make something. have a social interaction.* broad, open-ended, tiny steps leave room for success. set the bar so low you can't possibly miss it!

for a long, long time i was stuck. lost. definitely not RISING, definitely not shining. even though it is what i longed to do... and what i felt like i *should* do... i just couldn't.

simply surviving was my purpose.

but then, slowly slowly i felt ready. i began to become sick of my own stuckness, bored of the same old darkness day in and day out. i got tired of my own sad story... i was ready to write the next chapter.

and that is when the baby steps really began to lead me somewhere... to grow into bigger steps... to feel like moving forward was finally possible.

i won't begin to pretend i know what it feels like for you when you find yourself in the darkness... we all have our own unique experiences which we must honour. but i know for me, the last thing i wanted was someone telling me: *you should just try this... you should go do that.*

because every single thing that might have helped, that might have made me feel better... i avoided, i resisted, i gave up. it doesn't make sense, but that is how it can feel in the black hole of the darkness.

if you are in a dark place right now i want to honour that space with you.

i do not want to be one of those people who says 'do this'. because it is hard. it's individual. and it's your experience to honour.

but please know this: i see you. and i climb into the cave to sit beside you.

and if there is anything at all that *you* can do for you — even the tiniest bits of kindling that might offer the tiniest of sparks — know that it is a start, and that it is enough.

now it's your turn...

how will you move forward?

what are you struggling with? what strategies could you try? what will be your next step?

and what difference might it make in your life?

you picked up this book because you are feeling stuck with something. what would it be like for you to not be stuck anymore? how would you feel to actually have that stuff shift in your life? what would it be like if your windows weren't all clouded over by that fog... how might your light shine then?

and what if you don't get unstuck? what if you put this book on a shelf to gather dust? what if you just walk away without trying a single strategy and carry on as you always have? what if you don't RISE from this place?

what will that feel like for you? imagine the pain of staying in this stuck place... imagine still being stuck a year from now. five years from now. ten years from now. feeling the same things you are feeling now: uncertain, afraid, unworthy... frustrated, ashamed, disconnected, dejected... lost, powerless, small, dim.

ugh. i hope that picture in your head feels really awful. it does to me... the thought of you staying in that stuck, small, same place breaks my heart... the thought of you not shining your light in the world feels tragic to me. i hope it does to you too. in order to really make a change, the pain of staying exactly where you are has to outweigh the pain of change.

so that snapshot that you just created in your head... hang onto it. let it be the contrast that drives you take action and shift the stuckness you feel.

it's your time to RISE.

look to the sun.

i have one last strategy to share with you. i saved this one for last because i think it is a simple, quick, yet powerful way to anchor into the energy of what we are here to do: to get unstuck, to move forward, to RISE.

think about the sun: it never lets you down... every single day it sets. every single day it rises.

even on the dreariest of days, covered by dark clouds or think fog, the sun still rises.

the sun rises again and again... and so shall you.

let the sun be a reminder to you... a symbol, a sign, or an anchor: you are a riser, now act like it!

use the setting or the rising of the sun to empower your soul: create a daily sunrise or sunset practice.

(it's your choice on which; do what appeals to you, and also what actually fits into your life.)

where i am located, my front porch looks out towards the sea and the sunset, so i am very lucky to have a beautiful sunset right out my door every night. i am also not a morning person – i know myself, i am never going to be out there to experience the sun rise!

but *you* might love to catch a sunrise. you might also love a good sunset. you can mix this practice up and do both!

you might not be able to do this every day... you can simply try to fit a few more sunrises and sunsets into your week or month.

i suggest you set the alarm on your phone in advance, just to be sure you catch the sunrise or sunset and actually make time for this.

it only takes a few minutes... and these might become a juicy few minutes in your day... you may begin to crave this practice!

i also suggest taking a photo of your sunrise or sunset — post it to your favourite social media.

even if there is a day that you can't catch the sunrise or sunset, just looking at the images you have captured can still evoke this same energy.

here is the idea, whether you focus on the sunset or the sunrise...

when the sun sets or rises take this moment to go stand outdoors (if possible) or to simply look outside, to face the sunset or sunrise.

stand with your bare feet (if possible) grounded to the earth.

as the sun sinks into or rises up from the earth remember that mother earth is always supporting you. trust in that. anchor into that support.

stand with your arms, and your heart, open. as you look towards the light of the sun, remember that the divine light of spirit is always embracing you. trust in that. connect to that source of light.

stand tall and strong. as you feel the warmth of the sun on your *self*, remember the light of your soul. connect to your *self*. trust in your *self*.

if the sun is setting now, remember this:

tomorrow the sun will rise again, and so shall i.

if the sun is rising now, remember this:

just as the sun rises today, so shall i.

remember...

just like the sun, i am a RISER.

never forget that.

***

play more: share your sunrise and sunset photos with the hashtag #iamariser — we can all soak up the energy you share... we can all have a little reminder in our day to remember: i am a riser!

acknowledgements.

there was a time that i thought this book would never see the light of day... it would become a thing i wrote once that just disappeared in the cloud. the one thing that made me unearth it and revisit it was the promise i made to my mom to finish it. at a time when i felt that i had lost my self and lost my direction, something inside of me kept whispering: *finish the book, it is your next step.* and that was enough to keep me moving forwards, having one next step to take.

i am thankful to everyone who encouraged me to keep writing, to keep sharing, to keep shining... especially at a time when i didn't feel very shiny at all.

i am extremely grateful to the beta readers who provided early feedback about the book — your enthusiasm for the different strategies helped me believe that this book that i was writing for me and for my mom would indeed help others too.

i owe so much to those who do the work of helping people get unstuck: who write books, and make podcasts, and build communities in the service of helping others rise and shine. i thank you for teaching and inspiring me... i pledge to keep learning and to contribute to the collective library that helps us all. after all, we've got work to do.

about the author.

karen gunton is an unstucktor, a light igniter, and a badass rule-breaker who never uses capitals. she is on a mission to inspire others to seek their purpose and shine their light in the world. she started the light-house revolution as a  call to action for those who wish to gete unstuck and start living a life that lights them up.

she lives in adelaide, australia with her husband and three children... though, every australian winter she chases the sun back to canada for some more summer fun. you can find her in her happy place: on the beach with a book in one hand, a cold beer in the other, and her bare toes in the sand.

find karen on facebook, instagram, and twitter @karengunton or at her website karengunton.com where you will find free resources for people who are ready to rise up out of their stuckness and shine their light.

get more.

get unstuck – an online mini-workshop. create your own personal, powerful RISING practice to get unstuck from any muddy puddle you might be in!

hero's journey – still stuck? an online mini-workshop to explore your journey for the pitfalls that may be keeping you stuck and learn the best way forward.

visit karengunton.com

illuminate: the lighthouse oracle — get curious, tune into your intuition, explore the layers of your stuckness.

lighthouse revolution book + companion workbook **navigate** — build the lighthouse that will help you shine your light in the world

references.

[1] Doyle, Glennon. *Untamed: Stop Pleasing, Start Living.* Vermilion, 2020. Print.
[2] *Supernatural.* The CW, 2006-2020. Television.
[3] Rumi. *Selected Poems.* Penguin UK, 2015. Print.
[4] Bernstein, Gabrielle. "We can't live in the Light All the Time… But We Can Come Back Fast." gabbybernstein.com. February 2018. Web.
[5] *The Marvelous Mrs. Maisel.* Prime Video, 2017-2020. Television.
[6] Lamott, Anne. *Bird by Bird: Some Instructions on Writing and Life.* Anchor, 1994. Print.
[7] Rogers, Fred. *Mr Rogers Neighborhood.* PBS, 1971-2001. Television.
[8] Schucman, Helen. *A Course in Miracles.* Foundation for Inner Peace, 1975. Print.
[9] Bernstein, Gabrielle. "A Lesson in Practicing Acceptance and Remembering Your True Purpose." gabbybernstein.com. February 2019. Web.
[10] Brooks, Garth. *Standing Outside the Fire, In Pieces.* Liberty Records, 1993.
[11] Radmacher, Mary Anne. *Simply An Inspired Life: Consciously Choosing Unbounded Happiness in Good Times & Bad.* Conari Press, 2009. Print.
[12] Platten, Rachel. *Fight Song, Fight Song.* Columbia Records, 2015.
[13] Morrisey, Mary. *The Hidden Code for Transforming Dreams into Reality.* TEDx Wilmington Women, 2016. Web.
[14] Robbins, Mel. *The 5 Second Rule: Transform Your Life, Work, and Confidence with Everyday Courage.* Savio Republic, 2017. Print.
[15] Brown, Brené. *Brené on FFTs, Unlocking Us with Brené Brown.* brenébrown.com, March 2020. Podcast.
[16] Indigo Girls. *Closer to Fine, Indigo Girls.* Epic Records, 1989.

resources.

karengunton.com:
illuminate: the lighthouse oracle
lighthouse keepers digital magazine
lighthouse revolution playlist + RISE playlist
meet the lighthouse keepers
meet your shadow hunter
meet your inner child
meet your future self
cord cutting
intro to tapping + tap to get unstuck

books:
the secret language of your body, inna segal
you can heal your life, louise hay
rise sister rise, rebecca campbell
emotions & essential oils, enlighten alternative healing
change me prayers, tosha silver
untamed: stop pleasing, start living, glennon doyle
the big leap, gay hendricks
the little book of still, annie Harvey, thestilleffect.com.au

web:
unlocking us podcast, brene brown, brenebrown.com
tap with brad, brad yates, youtube
yoga with adrienne, youtube
psychic strengths quiz, deniselitchfield.com
sanctuary, helenjoybutler.com
healing with ho'oponnopono, joe vitale, youtube
universal cycles of change, nataliesisson.com
stages of grief and _finding meaning_, david kessler, grief.com

play more: do you have favourite resources and tools for getting unstuck and RISING? do share using the hashtag #iamariser ...i am always learning and would love to hear from you.

rise.

www.ingramcontent.com/pod-product-compliance
Lightning Source LLC
Chambersburg PA
CBHW070418010526
44118CB00014B/1810